CAMPAIGN • 207

SOLFERINO 1859

The battle for Italy's freedom

Feldmarschall-Leutnant Benedek führt in der Schlacht bei Solferino am 24. Juni 1859 das Infanterie-Regiment „Dom Miguel" zum Sturm.

RICHARD BROOKS

ILLUSTRATED BY PETER DENNIS

Series editors Marcus Cowper and Nikolai Bogdanovic

First published in Great Britain in 2009 by Osprey Publishing,
PO Box 883, Oxford, OX1 9PL, UK
PO Box 3985, New York, NY 10185-3985, USA
Email: info@ospreypublishing.com

Osprey Publishing is part of the Osprey Group.

Transferred to digital print on demand 2014.

First published 2009
2nd impression 2010

Printed and bound by
Cadmus Communications, USA.

A CIP catalogue record for this book is available from the
British Library.

ISBN: 978 1 84603 385 8
PDF e-book ISBN: 978 1 84603 874 7

Editorial by Ilios Publishing Ltd, Oxford, UK
   (www.iliospublishing.com)
Page layout by The Black Spot
Index by Michael Forder
Typeset in Sabon and Myriad Pro
Maps by Bounford.com
3D bird's-eye views by The Black Spot
Battlescene illustrations by Peter Dennis
Originated by United Graphic Pte Ltd, Singapore

The Woodland Trust
Osprey Publishing is supporting the Woodland Trust, the UK's
leading woodland conservation charity, by funding the
dedication of trees.

www.ospreypublishing.com

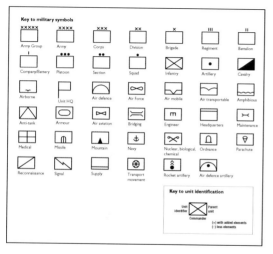

Key to military symbols

Acknowledgements
The author would like to thank Ken Brooks, Dave Carson,
Stephen Courtenay, Ian Drury, David Isby, Jeff James, Charles
and Ruth Matthieson, Piero Pompili and Ralph Weaver for their
invaluable assistance.

Sources of illustrations are shown as follows:

Abbreviation	Publication
Bossoli	*The War in Italy*
lemonde	*Le Monde Illustré*
ILN	*Illustrated London News*
Miller	*Study of the Italian Campaign*
INW	*Illustrated News of the World*
photo	*Original photograph June 2008*
Voss	*Geschichte der Deutschen Einigungskriege*

Copyright is 'Author' or 'RNM', Royal Naval Museum,
Portsmouth, as shown.

Senior ranks

Command	Austrian	French	Sardinian
Army	*Feldmarschall* (FM) *General der Kavallerie* (GderK) *Feldzeugmeister* (FZM)	*Maréchal*	*Generale*
Corps or division	*Feld-Marschall-Leutnant* (FML)	*Général de division*	*luogotenente generale*
Brigade	*General-Major* (GM)	*Général de brigade*	*maggior generale*

Glossary

Adjutantenkorps	Austrian Staff Corps
l'Armée d'Afrique	French forces based in Algeria
Cacciatori delle Alpi	Riflemen of the Alps, i.e. Garibaldi's volunteers
Chasseur à pied	French light infantryman
Chasseur à cheval	French light cavalryman
Chasseur d'Afrique	French light cavalryman recruited from European soldiers of fortune for service in Africa
Grenztruppen	Austrian border troops recruited in Croatia, shortened to Grenzer
Hussar	Austrian, or French light cavalryman
Jäger	Austrian light infantry recruited in the Tyrol
Lignard	French line infantry soldier
pas de charge	the charge
Pdr	weight of shot fired by artillery piece
SB	smooth bore
tête-du-pont	bridgehead
Tirailleur Algérien	French light infantry soldier recruited from Algeria's Arab population
Turco	Popular term for a Tirailleur Algérien
Voltigeur	type of French Guard infantryman
Zouave	French light infantry recruited from European soldiers of fortune, wearing an Algerian style of uniform

CONTENTS

INTRODUCTION

The battle of Solferino was fought on 24 June 1859, just south of Lake Garda in northern Italy. It ended a two-month campaign that saw the first large-scale use of railways in war, and the first battlefield deployment of rifled field artillery. Overshadowed by subsequent bloodier conflicts, the Italian campaign was the single most important step in the development of the infantry tactics of World War I. It provided soldiers of the American Civil War with their latest images of modern war, both sides adopting the glamorous French *zouave* uniforms, while their drill manuals admitted their indebtedness to French practice.

Solferino and the associated action at San Martino provided a major impetus towards Italian unification. It was the largest battle fought on European soil since Leipzig at the end of the Napoleonic Wars. It drew in over a quarter of a million men: French and Italians on one side, the polyglot forces of the Habsburg Empire, known collectively as Austrians, on the other. Over 26,000 men were killed or wounded in a single day, carnage that inspired the formation of the International Red Cross.

The conflict's underlying causes were the determination of every French Government since 1815 to overthrow the treaties that ended the Napoleonic Wars, and the unhappy situation of Italy. Italy in 1859 was a geographical rather than a political expression, divided between half a dozen Italian-ruled states, and an Austrian-occupied area in the north-east. An old-fashioned dynastic empire with its capital at Vienna, Austria was held together by the figure of the emperor or Kaiser. Sprawling from Milan in the west to the Carpathian Mountains in the east, the empire included Germans, Magyars, Czechs, Italians and Poles, besides innumerable minor nationalities. It had everything to fear from the forces of nationalism released by the French Revolution. A large Austrian army had occupied

Vittorio Emmanuele II, king of Sardinia, and his son Prince Umberto of Piedmont. Italy was a fragmented patchwork of minor states, until Solferino started the process of bringing them together around Sardinia and Piedmont. (Author/INW)

Lombardy and Venice since 1815, as a bastion against renewed French aggression. Most of the rest of Italy was a patchwork of despotic minor states dependent on Austrian bayonets. The presence of Habsburg troops outraged Italian national sentiment and damaged the economy. Ladies in Milan wore black, as if in mourning, and refused to dance with Austrian army officers, while Austrian repression alienated otherwise apolitical groups.

French troops at Solferino: a re-established Garde Impériale about to overthrow the European settlement imposed on France by the victors of the Napoleonic Wars. (Author/Bossoli)

The only threat to Austria's position came from a political entity that was itself only half Italian. The Kingdom of Sardinia was not based in the island of that name, but in the Alpine passes of Savoy and the plains of Piedmont around Turin, hence the expression 'Piedmontese' often used instead of Sardinian. Sardinia had led an Italian uprising against the Habsburgs during Europe's 'Year of Revolutions' in 1848, but Graf Johann Radetzky, Austria's viceroy in Milan, crushed the revolt in battles at Custozza and Novara. Sardinia's new king, Vittorio Emmanuele II, doggedly rebuilt his forces, however. He sent troops to help the British and French during the Crimean War, gaining a place at the 1856 peace conference, where Italy's problems appeared firmly on the agenda. During the summer of 1858, Vittorio Emmanuele's Prime Minister, Conte Camillo di Cavour, negotiated secretly with Napoleon III, the French head of state. Nephew of the great emperor, Napoleon III had ruled a revived French Empire since 1852, and was anxious to overturn the 1815 settlement. In return for help against Austria, Sardinia would cede its French-speaking areas of Savoy and Nice to France.

Propaganda image of the French emperor Napoleon III: nephew of the great Napoleon and political adventurer, he was also an authority on artillery, giving his name to the standard field piece of the American Civil War. (Author/lemonde)

Napoleon III sparked off a crisis in January 1859, with a few undiplomatic words to the Austrian ambassador at a New Year's reception. The Sardinians concentrated their army along the border with Lombardy. The French Army bought horses and stockpiled supplies, while their arsenals manufactured thousands of cartridges for newly issued rifled cannon and muskets. The Austrian Government reinforced their Zweite Armee, recalling 65,000 men from furlough. In early April they sent another army corps to Italy. Austrian infantry regiments began calling up their reservists. Sardinia promptly called out her own reserves, and armed her fortresses at Casale and Alessandria. Volunteers were enlisted and irregular forces formed under the famous revolutionary Giuseppe Garibaldi, regarded by conservatives as a terrorist.

Some of Garibaldi's volunteers (left to right): officer, light cavalryman, infantryman and officer in campaign dress. The Garibaldini of 1859 exchanged their trademark red shirts for conventional Sardinian uniforms, to placate socially conservative Italian nationalists. (Author/INW)

Over 14,000 recruits came forward from the rest of Italy, men whom the Sardinians would find it difficult to disown if the crisis were defused.

The Austrian Foreign Minister, Graf Ferdinand von Buol-Schauenstein, ensured it was not. A Bavarian minister once described him as a locomotive that didn't know where it was going, responding to enquiries by blowing steam and whistling. Buol did not believe Napoleon was serious. He prevented Austria making effective military preparations, while adopting a tough attitude that made war inevitable. Convinced the Sardinians were bluffing, Buol issued an ultimatum demanding their immediate unilateral disarmament. As late as 18 April, a nervous Napoleon had been insisting the Sardinians back down, but Buol's ultimatum, presented on 22 April, changed all that. Before its formal rejection on the 26th, French troops entered Savoy, pre-empting the threatened Austrian invasion by three days. Three troop trains passed Chambéry on the way to St Jean de Maurienne on 25 April, the slogan 'Excursion to Italy' chalked on their carriages. More followed. None of the great powers moved to help the Austrians who had precipitated war when diplomatic victory was in their grasp. It soon appeared that Austria was no better equipped for the impending military confrontation than she had been for the preceding political manoeuvres.

CHRONOLOGY

April

23   Austrian ultimatum demands Sardinian disarmament

25   French troop trains enter Piedmont

26   Sardinia rejects Austrian ultimatum

29   Austrians cross river Ticino

May

8   Austrians approach Turin, Piedmontese retreat south of river Po

9   French join Piedmontese at Alessandria, Austrians withdraw across river Sesia

10   Napoleon III leaves Paris, arrives Alessandria on 14th

20   French defeat Austrian reconnaissance at Montebello

21–24   Piedmontese troops probe across Po at Vercelli and Casale

24   Garibaldi enters Austrian territory, and defeats Austrians at Varese on 26th

28   Allies begin flank march on Novara, through Casale and Vercelli

29   Urban reoccupies Varese

30   Piedmontese cross Sesia at Prarolo, and capture Palestro and Confienza

31   Austrian counterattacks on Palestro and Confienza defeated

31   Garibaldi defeated at Laveno

June

1   French advance guard reaches Novara

2   Austrian Army retreats over Ticino, I Korps arrives at Magenta

3   Austrians move on Magenta; French cross Ticino at Turbigo, and take Robechetto

4   Battle of Magenta

5   Austrians retreat on Milan and Melegnano

6   Austrians evacuate Milan, which the Allies enter next day

8   French attack Austrian rearguard at Melegnano

9–16   Austrians fall back on river Chiese, followed by the Allies

17   Gyulai resigns Austrian command

18   Austrian forces split into two armies, under Franz Josef's personal command

21   Austrians withdraw across river Mincio

22   Allies cross Chiese, and advance to Castiglione

23   Austrians recross Mincio

24   Battles of Solferino and San Martino

27   Austrians abandon Mincio, and withdraw into the Quadrilateral

28   French cross Mincio, while Piedmontese invest Peschiera

July

2   Austrians initiate peace talks with Napoleon III

7   Armistice agreed leading to Peace of Villa Franca and Treaty of Zürich on 10 November

OPPOSING COMMANDERS

The Austrian Kaiser Franz Josef ruled the multi-ethnic Habsburg Empire in central Europe from 1848 to 1916. Solferino began a process of destabilization that ended with the empire's collapse after World War I. (Author/Voss)

AUSTRIAN

The Austrian Army of 1859 was commanded by a narrow aristocratic clique dominated by the **Kaiser Franz Josef**, who surrounded himself with deferential aristocrats, who shared his own narrow views. Obsessed with the petty detail of army regulations, he could not understand the social and military changes of his day, believing that his army depended not on learned officers, but on brave and chivalrous gentlemen.

Chief amongst these was **Graf Karl Ludwig Grünne**, the Kaiser's personal Adjutant-General. With little military experience, Grünne systematically undermined the professional structure of the army. He dispensed with the Minister of War, and humiliated the Chief of Staff, **Quarter-Master-General FML Baron Heinrich Hess**[1]. Credited with Radetzky's victory at Novara, Hess was the best strategic mind in the Austrian Army. When Franz Josef took personal command in Italy in June 1859 he took both Grünne and Hess with him, ensuring continued friction. Until then, Austrian forces in Italy, known as Zweite Armee, were commanded by **FZM Graf Franz Gyulai**. A friend of Grünne, one of Gyulai's first actions had been to order all soldiers to wear black whiskers. The fair haired and unwhiskered had to dye their moustaches, or stain their upper lips with boot polish. Gyulai had few illusions about his abilities, asking to be relieved on the outbreak of war. However, he ignored advice from better-qualified officers. His relations with **Oberst Franz Kuhn**, his capable chief of staff, were so bad they communicated in writing. A staff officer commented that the confusion at headquarters made him ill.

The Austrian officer corps reflected the social prejudices of the high command. Commissions went to those who could afford them. Promotion was in the hands of regimental proprietors who were influenced by social rather than professional considerations. A contemporary described **FZM Graf Wimpffen**, commander of Erste Armee at Solferino, as, 'one of those Austrian generals whose nature it was, in Suvarov's phrase, to be beaten'. Only **FML Ludwig von Benedek** of VIII Korps shines out, with his eagle glance and fiery energy. Unlike most Austrian commanders Benedek was a fighting general with an instinctive understanding of the battlefield and an unusual empathy with the ordinary soldier. After the hard fighting of 1848–49, most senior Austrian officers were glad to get back to peacetime routine. Their subordinates were frivolous, snobbish and ignorant. When

---

1 See the list of senior ranks (page 2) for senior Austrian ranks shown here in abbreviated form, e.g.FML, etc.

introduced to *Kriegspiel*, the wargame that prepared Prussian officers for their victories in 1866 and 1870, the Austrian response was to enquire how to win money at it. The Staff was a means of providing jobs for favourite officers, without risking their skins. Radetzky described them as *Glückpilze* or happy mushrooms. As part of his attack on the military establishment Grünne invented a parallel command system, the *Adjutantenkorps*. Its officers reported directly to him, outranked their operational staff equivalents, and counter-signed the latter's orders, creating delay and confusion.

FRENCH

Described in a contemporary newspaper as belonging to 'the juvenile irregular school', the French commander-in-chief **Napoleon III** owed his position to his wits. He would adopt any means, however unconventional, to justify his claim to his uncle's throne. Lacking formal military experience, Napoleon III's personal energy and intellectual interest in military affairs contrasts sharply with the complacent ignorance of his opponent. His ability to be in the right place, shaking hands with smoke-blackened *zouaves*, or having an epaulette shot off at Solferino, gave him an operational authority absent on the other side.

Feldzeugmeister Graf Franz Gyulai, Austrian commander-in-chief in Italy at the start of the war. A well-connected Hungarian aristocrat, he lacked operational experience, and was out of his depth as an army commander. (RNM/ILN)

Unlike the Austrians, who were notorious for their low level of officer casualties in action, French officers led from in front. Corps commanders had all seen active service, some as long ago as the Napoleonic Wars. **Baraguey d'Hilliers** of I Corps had lost a hand at Leipzig. **Général Regnaud de St Jean d'Angély** of the Guard had suffered so many wounds he declared himself no longer a man but a bit of lace. Younger officers had fought in Algeria or in the Crimean War. The only weak link was Napoleon III's lamentable cousin **Prince Napoleon** at V Corps, known as 'Craint Plomb', or 'Fears Lead', following an early departure from the Crimea after the battle of the Alma.

Senior French officers were usually graduates of the military academies of St Cyr or the Polytéchnique, although Napoleonic traditions of centralization often cramped their initiative. Many regimental officers, however, were ex-rankers, promoted for long service or bravery in action. Such men provided a cohesion and professional expertise lacking among Austrian cadres.

Feld-Marschall-Leutnant Ludwig von Benedek, charismatic commander of Austrian VIII Korps and victor of Solferino's twin battle at San Martino. (Author/Voss)

SARDINIAN

Vittorio Emmanuele fought as a divisional commander in 1848–49, and would have happily remained a regimental officer all his life. One of his proudest distinctions was to be elected honorary corporal by the 3e Zouaves, after accompanying them into action at Palestro. The brain behind the Sardinian armed forces was the Minister of War, **Generale Alfonso La Marmora**, who rebuilt the army in the 1850s, and accompanied Vittorio Emmanuele throughout the 1859 campaign. La Marmora's first reform had been to purge the many Sardinian officers who failed at Novara. He set up infantry and cavalry schools to train replacements, and employed competent soldiers of fortune from other Italian armies, taking the first step towards a unified Italian officer corps. One man who would do more than anyone to create a unified Italy was of course **Garibaldi**. Once condemned to death by the Sardinian authorities for revolutionary activities, in 1859 he was commissioned into the Sardinian Army to rally support for the cause.

OPPOSING FORCES

AUSTRIAN

The armies about to confront one another upon the Lombard plain were all recruited by conscription, although none had yet extended the burdens of military service to all levels of society. This was particularly true of the Austrians whose other ranks consisted largely of illiterate peasants. Recruits served only two or three years with the colours, before being furloughed to save money. When recalled they were practically untrained and no match for the French. Drawn from a multinational empire, the Austrian Army recognized ten different languages for regimental purposes. Soldiers learnt only a few basic words of German, the army's unified command language. Many officers spoke to their men through interpreters. Different nationalities were often antagonistic or disaffected. Hungarian officers reduced to the ranks after fighting for independence in 1848–49 provided a particular focus for discontent.

Neglected by their officers, Austrian soldiers fought out of duty, in a spirit of resignation, losing enormous numbers of prisoners in every action.

Austrian Army uniforms: officers talking to a dismounted hussar (centre), line infantry in white tunics and border troops in darker shades (left), and a rifleman in his Tyrolean *Jäger* hat (right). Mounted figures include an *Uhlan* (lancer) and a dragoon in white. (Author/lemonde)

A contemporary critic wrote: 'Once the machine was derailed, once the ranks broken and the officers down, it seemed to the Austrian soldier that he had finished his work; in the French army on the other hand, it is only then that the soldier really starts his work.'

Every aspect of the Austrian soldier's life was regulated in obsessive detail. He was very good at massed manoeuvres on the parade ground, but hopeless at the open order fighting required in the broken terrain of northern Italy.

The Austrians had possessed some very good light infantry corps raised in the Tyrol and Croatia, known as *Jäger* and *Grenztruppen* respectively. These traditional sources of skirmishers had been allowed to atrophy since 1848–49. The Croats in particular were regarded as politically unreliable, demonstrating the weakness of an army whose internal security role demanded loyalty before combat effectiveness.

Light infantry were important in 1859 as a way of counteracting the increased lethality of firearms. Infantry muskets were still loaded via the muzzle, as they had been in the Napoleonic Wars, but they had seen two major improvements. Percussion caps placed over a nipple and exploded by a hammer had replaced the old flintlock system, dramatically reducing misfires. Various systems, most notably the expanding bullet invented in the early 1850s by Captain Claude Minié of the French Army, allowed muzzle-loading rifles to be fired as quickly as smoothbore muskets, but with an effective range of 365m instead of 45m. Edged weapons would cause only 1.67 per cent of the casualties suffered during the Italian campaign.

Military critics claimed the new rifles were fragile and complicated, and they may have been right. Magenta and Solferino bucked the trend towards tactical stalemate established in the Crimea and repeated in the American Civil War. This was partly because Austrian infantry made poor use of their new 13mm-calibre Lorenz rifles. Many received theirs on the way to the front, and had never fired them on the range. Some Austrian battalions still had smoothbore 'Augustin' muskets, with rifles issued only to designated sharpshooters. Austrian officers often regarded musketry training as an excuse for a picnic. Not surprisingly it was said that, outside the specialist *Jäger* battalions, Austrian soldiers shot like pigs.

Austrian artillery still used smoothbore guns, firing a mixture of round shot and case. It had too few draught horses, the pieces were heavy and lacked mobility. They also used rockets, ranging up to 1,600 paces (1,200m), whose main achievement at Solferino was frightening their own infantry. The increased range of firearms was eroding cavalry's role on the battlefield, and made reconnaissance a problem for both sides. In peacetime Austrian cavalry practised spectacular charges that impressed foreign observers, but had little tactical value in the field.

Austrian logistics were another weak area. Their defensive posture enabled them to hold large quantities of food in magazines based in fortresses, but the rations issued to the troops were insufficient. Austrian soldiers received only one cooked meal per day, often fighting on empty stomachs. Units suffered heavy wastage from exhaustion and hunger, exacerbated by lack of tents. The Austrians either billeted their troops among a hostile population swarming with spies, or roughed it in the open, suffering widespread sickness. Either way, discipline suffered, with frequent allegations of looting and worse. For most of the campaign, the Austrians struggled along in full kit until, just before Solferino, Franz Josef ordered their knapsacks to be carried in wagons, further impairing their mobility.

FRENCH

Magenta and Solferino are often described as 'soldiers' battles', making the differences between the opposing armies' rank and file unusually important. The French made better use of available manpower, despite a popular reaction against the swollen armies of the First Empire, and the mass slaughter they had encouraged. Since 1815 only a quarter of young Frenchmen had served their seven years with the colours. Many old soldiers re-enlisted as paid substitutes for middle-class youths who drew a bad number in the annual lottery. Consequently a third of French infantrymen were long-service regulars.

French regulations and practice left a great deal to the troops, who possessed a natural talent for skirmishing. This was especially so in the new light infantry units: the *zouaves* and *chasseurs à pied*. Such troops did not skirmish just to distract the enemy or screen the battle line. For them fighting in extended order meant independent groups of men creeping up under cover to disrupt the enemy with an unexpected burst of fire, or suddenly appearing on his flank in a great swarm. General George B. McClellan of the US Army thought that, of all the troops he saw in Europe, it would be the greatest honour to assist in defeating the *zouaves*. Many rising French commanders had served in these units. Maréchau François Canrobert of III Corps and Patrice MacMahon of II Corps had both commanded *chasseur* battalions, MacMahon sacrificing seven years' seniority to do so.

French light and line infantry units shared a cult of the bayonet. This benefited from two circumstances: their opponents' poor marksmanship and the high trajectory typical of muzzle-loading rifles, which sent bullets whizzing harmlessly overhead, unless sights were set just right. French tactics emphasized a rapid advance, closing with the bayonet before the enemy could adjust their sights. A *chasseur* who fought at Magenta claimed his battalion took lots of prisoners, without firing a shot. Line and light infantry had different types of rifle, the latter using shorter weapons, known as 'carabines'. Some metropolitan French line battalions are said to have had smoothbore muskets,

Formal tactics followed earlier patterns, although Napoleon III had recently reorganized his infantry, cutting the number of ranks from three to two, with six companies per battalion instead of eight. This reduced depth, and hence vulnerability to rifle fire. In the Crimea single Minié balls had been known to penetrate several Russians in succession. Nevertheless, infantry battalions still manoeuvred in columns of companies, or double companies on open ground. A brigade of five, six or seven battalions might form two lines of battalion columns at deployment intervals, leaving space between them for the units in front to form line. Between a sixth

French *zouaves* and battle honours they won before, during, and after the Italian campaign. Their African or 'Turkish' style of dress with its baggy trousers and short open jacket was imitated by both Union and Confederate regiments. (Author/postcard)

French artillery on railway trucks at Susa on the Piedmontese side of the Alps. The Italian campaign saw the first use in a major war of both railways and rifled field guns. (Author/INW)

and a third of the men acted as skirmishers, screening the main body. In the French Army they often led the way into the enemy position. On the defensive such a deployment allowed the first line to break up an enemy charge by fire, leaving surviving attackers vulnerable to counterattack by the second line. These advanced in column with drums beating, passing through the gaps left in the front line by companies detached as skirmishers. When ground permitted, the French sometimes reverted to the massive columns of the First Empire, stacking battalions three deep to provide an assault formation 18 ranks deep.

The French artillery was the first in the world to employ rifled guns, converted from existing smoothbore weapons using the La Hitte system. Improved manufacturing techniques had increased artillery ranges already, but rifling instantly doubled ranges and accuracy. The lower muzzle velocity of rifled guns also improved their usefulness. Their more curved trajectory allowed them to fire over intervening lines of infantry, like howitzers, although the new conical shells sometimes failed to explode. The close terrain of the war's early actions made it hard to assess the value of the new guns, which could not fire case shot, the traditional close-range artillery weapon, without stripping their rifling. Solferino's more open terrain allowed the French to mass their guns to knock out Austrian batteries with long-range shell fire. French artillery tactics were as dynamic as under the first Napoleon, guns advancing from one firing position to another as the action progressed.

Most of the French cavalry present during the campaign were light, known variously as *hussards* and *chasseurs à cheval*. Realizing cavalry's problems with reconnaissance, the French also deployed balloons filled with coal gas. The only gas supply was in major towns, however, and the balloons deflated before reaching anywhere they might have been useful. The campaign's most important technical novelty was the steam engine. Napoleon's effective use of railways and steamships negated the Austrian's initial advantage in numbers, and then allowed him to seize the strategic initiative, nearly ending the campaign at a stroke.

The French generally had plenty of food, although there was not always time to cook it. Their convoys choked the line of march, and could have caused problems if any retreat had been necessary. Generally they made better campaigners, issuing coffee before marching off and sleeping in the shelter

Sardinian uniforms: dismounted figures from the left – a light cavalryman, three infantrymen, a seated rifleman from the elite *bersaglieri* in their feathered hat, an engineer, a heavy cavalryman and *carabiniere*, and a gunner. (Author/lemonde)

tents that every man carried. Before the campaign began, Napoleon lightened his soldiers' load, restricting their kit to greatcoat, trousers, two pairs of boots and a kepi, the peaked forage cap that became the French soldier's trademark, and was widely adopted in the American Civil War. Only the Guard kept its full-dress bearskins and shakoes. *Généraux* abandoned their cocked hats, while officers rolled their rations in an overcoat worn bandolier fashion. Everything else was left behind at the French base in Genoa.

SARDINIAN

Sardinia's conscription system focussed on quantity rather than quality, although their four-year term was still longer than the actual service of most Austrian conscripts. Despite their short service the Sardinians did well in the Crimea. General McClellan compared their discipline and appearance with the best troops in Europe. Like their allies the Sardinians were nationally homogenous, sharing a common language, interests and customs, drawing on a wider cross section of society than the Austrians. They too had formed specialist light infantry, known as *bersaglieri*, armed with a short rifle known as the Carabina modello 1856. Sardinian line infantry used a mixture of their own and French smoothbore weapons, and British rifles bought in the months before the war. Tactics resembled the French, though they rarely succeeded in massing their forces as the French did. Among his other reforms La Marmora formed new light cavalry units, better suited to Italy's broken terrain than heavy cavalry. These combined a reconnaissance and a tactical battlefield role, charging gallantly at Montebello and San Martino.

ORDERS OF BATTLE

AUSTRIAN ARMY

Austrian forces in northern Italy were completely reorganized between the battles of Magenta and Solferino. Separate orders of battle, therefore, are given for the two actions. Austrian battalions (bns) mobilized six companies of up to 236 men. In practice heavy losses on the march reduced this to about 130 in the field. Heavy or light cavalry regiments had six or eight squadrons (sqns) respectively of 120 sabres. Artillery batteries had six SB guns, generally 6-pdr and two 7-pdr SB howitzers. Brigades were known by their commander's surname. Names following the number of an infantry regiment (IR) indicate the regimental proprietor or *Inhaber*, i.e. the colonel-in-chief. Line regiments fielded four battalions, forming a brigade by adding a light infantry battalion of *Jäger* or *Grenzer*. NB: figures in parentheses show actual numbers committed at Magenta.

MAGENTA, 4 JUNE 1859

Commander-in-chief – FZM Graf Gyulai
Chief of staff – Col Kuhn

I KORPS – FML GRAF EDOUARD CLAM GALLAS
(10,767 infantry, 24 guns)
1.Division – FML Montenuovo
Brigade Burdina (five bns and eight guns)
Jäger Bn. Nr. 2
IR Prinz Wasa Nr.60
Brigade Brunner (five bns and eight guns)
Grenz IR 2.Banal Nr.11 Bn.1
IR Graf Thun-Hohenstein Nr.29
2.Division – FML Cordon
Brigade Hoditz (five bns and eight guns)[1]
Jäger Bn. Nr.14
IR Erzherzog Ernst Nr.48
Brigade Reznicek (five bns and eight guns)
Grenz IR 2.Banal Nr.11 Bn.2
IR Erzherzog Josef Nr.37
Corps artillery (32 guns)

II KORPS – FML FÜRST LIECHTENSTEIN
(15,612 infantry, 519 cavalry, 48 guns)
1.Division – FML Jellaçic
Brigade Szabo (five bns and eight guns)[2]
Jäger Bn. Nr.7
IR Erzherzog Wilhelm Nr.12
Brigade Kudelka (five bns and eight guns)
Jäger Bn. Nr.21
IR Graf Jellaçic Nr.46
2.Division – FML Herdy
Brigade Baltin (five bns and eight guns)
Jäger Bn. Nr.10
IR Graf Hartmann-Klarstein Nr.9
Brigade Kintzl (four bns and eight guns)
IR Erzherzog Sigismund Nr.45

Corps artillery (16 guns)
Corps cavalry, Ulanenregiment Nr.12 (four sqns)

III KORPS – FML FÜRST SCHWARZENBERG
(20,391 infantry, 1,145 cavalry, 56 guns)
1.Division – FML Schönberger
Brigade Dürfeld (five bns and eight guns)
Jäger Bn. Nr.15
IR Erzherzog Stephan Nr.58
Brigade Ramming (five bns and eight guns)
Jäger Bn. Nr.13
IR König Leopold der Belgier Nr.27
2.Division – FML Martini
Brigade Wetzlar (five bns and eight guns)
Grenz IR Otocaner Nr.2 Bn.2
IR Fürst Liechtenstein Nr.5
Brigade Hartung (five bns and eight guns)
Jäger Bn. Nr.23
IR Grossherzog von Hesen Nr.14
Corps artillery (24 guns)
Corps cavalry, Husarenregiment Nr.10 (eight sqns)

V KORPS – FML GRAF STADION[3]
(24,452 infantry, 640 cavalry, 72 guns)
1.Division – FML Paumgarten
Brigade Gaal (five bns and eight guns)
Grenz IR Liccaner Nr.1 Bn.1
IR Erzherzog Karl Nr.3
Brigade Dormus (Hesse until Montebello)
(five bns and eight guns)
Jäger Bn. Nr.4
IR Baron Culoz Nr.31
Brigade Bils (five bns and eight guns)
Grenz IR Oguliner Nr.3 Bn.1
IR Graf Kinsky Nr.47
2.Division – FML Sternberg
Brigade Koller (five bns and eight guns)
Grenz IR Oguliner Nr.3 Bn.2
IR Herzog von Modena Nr.32
Brigade Festetics (five bns and eight guns)
Jäger Bn. Nr.6
IR Baron Reischach Nr.21
Corps artillery (32 guns)
Corps cavalry, Ulanenregiment Nr.12 (four sqns)

VII KORPS – FML BARON ZOBEL[4]
(15,464 infantry, 571 cavalry, 56 guns)
1.Division – FML Reischach
Brigade Lebzeltern (four bns and eight guns)
IR Kaiser Franz Josef Nr.1
Brigade Gablenz (five bns and eight guns)
Jäger Bn. Nr.3
IR Baron Grüber Nr.54
2.Division – FML Lilia
Brigade Weigl (four bns and eight guns)
IR Erzherzog Luitpold Nr.53
Brigade Dondorf (five bns and eight guns)
Grenz IR Otocaner Nr.2 Bn.1
IR Graf Wimpffen Nr.22

Corps artillery (24 guns)
Corps cavalry, Husarenregiment Nr.1 (four sqns)

VIII KORPS – FML GRAF BENEDEK[5]
(25,709 infantry, 626 cavalry, 72 guns)
1.Division – FML Berger
Brigade Varenemann (five bns and eight guns)
Jäger Bn. Nr.2
IR Baron Prohaska Nr.7
Brigade Roden (five bns and eight guns)
Grenz IR Szluiner Nr.4 Bn.2
IR Kronprinz Albrecht von Sachsen Nr.11
2.Division – FML Lang
Brigade Philipoviç (five bns and eight guns)
Jäger Bn. nr.5
IR Prinz Hohenlohe-Langenburg Nr.17
Brigade Boer (five bns and eight guns)
Jäger Bn. Nr.3
IR Dom Miguel Nr.39
Brigade Lippert (four bns and eight guns)
Jäger Bn. Nr.9
IR Erzherzog Rainer Nr.59
Corps artillery (32 guns)
Corps cavalry, Husarenregiment Nr.1 (four sqns)

IX KORPS – FML GRAF SCHAAFSGOTTSCHE[6]
(20,975 infantry, 428 cavalry, 56 guns)
1.Division – FML Handl
Brigade Castiglione (five bns and eight guns)
Grenz IR Gradiscaner Nr.8 Bn.2
IR Erzherzog Rudolf Nr.19
Brigade Braum (five bns and eight guns)
Grenz IR Gradiscaner Nr.8 Bn.1
IR Baron Rossbach Nr.40
Brigade Augustin (five bns and eight guns)
Jäger Bn. Nr.16
IR Prinz von Preussen Nr.34
2.Division – FML Crenneville
Brigade Blumencron (five bns and eight guns)
Jäger Bn. Nr.4
IR Erzherzog Franz Karl Nr.52
Brigade Fehlmayer (five bns and eight guns)
Grenzinfanteriebataillon Titler
IR Erzherzog Ludwig Nr.8
Corps artillery (24 guns)
Corps cavalry, Husarenregiment Nr.12 (four sqns)

Army artillery reserve (88 guns, 24 used)

Notes
1 Brigade not yet arrived.
2 Guns lost at Palestro.
3 Only Brigade Hess fought at Magenta
(4,120 infantry, eight guns).
4 Only 1.Division fought at Magenta
(7,293 infantry, 571 cavalry, 16 guns).
5 None of this corps was engaged at Magenta.
Brigade Boer was detached with Urban chasing
Garibaldi. Boer replaced GM Schaafsgottsche,
promoted to IX Korps.
6 None of this corps was engaged at Magenta.
Brigade Braum was detached with Urban.

SOLFERINO, 24 JUNE 1859

Commander-in-chief – His Imperial and Royal Highness Franz Josef
Chief of staff – FML Baron Hess
NB: figures in parentheses show actual numbers committed at Solferino. Formations marked with an asterisk saw no action.

Erste Armee – FZM Graf Wimpffen

II KORPS – FML FÜRST LIECHTENSTEIN*
(17,710 infantry, 450 cavalry, 56 guns)
1.Division – FML Jellaçic
Brigade Szabo (five bns and eight guns)
Grenz IR Nr.9 Peterwardeiner Bn.1
IR Erzherzog Wilhelm Nr.12
Brigade Wachter (five bns and eight guns)
Grenz IR Nr.10 1.Banal
IR Graf Jellaçic Nr.46
2.Division – FML Herdy
Brigade Kintzl (four bns)
IR Erzherzog Sigismund Nr.45
Brigade Hahn (six bns and eight guns)
4th Bns: IR Nr.21, 31, 32, 39, 47, 54
Corps artillery (32 guns)
Corps cavalry, Husarenregiment Nr.12 (four sqns)
Mantua Garrison attached (two-and-a-half bns)
4th Bns: IR Nr.1, 33, 49

III KORPS – FML FÜRST SCHWARZENBERG
(17,895 infantry, 880 cavalry, 72 guns)
1.Division – FML Schönberger
Brigade Pokorny (five bns and eight guns)
Jäger Bn. Nr.15
IR Erzherzog Stephan Nr.58
Brigade Dienstel (five bns and eight guns)
Jäger Bn. Nr.13
IR König Leopold der Belgier Nr.27
2.Division – FML Haberman
Brigade Wetzlar (five bns and eight guns)
Grenz IR Otocaner Nr.2 Bn.2
IR Fürst Liechtenstein Nr.5
Brigade Hartung (five bns and eight guns)
Jäger Bn. Nr.23
IR Grossherzog von Hesen Nr.14
Brigade Rösgen (five bns and eight guns)
Jäger Bn. Nr.7*
IR Baron Hess Nr.49
Corps artillery (32 guns)
Corps cavalry, Husarenregiment Nr.10 (eight sqns)

IX KORPS – GDERK GRAF SCHAAFSGOTTSCHE
(18,728 infantry, 480 cavalry, 64 guns)
1.Division – FML Handl
Brigade Castiglione (five bns and eight guns)
Grenz IR Gradiscaner Nr.8 Bn.2
IR Erzherzog Rudolf Nr.19
Brigade Wimpffen (five bns and eight guns)
Grenz IR Gradiscaner Nr.8 Bn.1*
IR Baron Rossbach Nr.40
Brigade Suini (five bns and eight guns)

Jäger Bn. Nr.16
IR Prinz von Preussen Nr.34
2.Division – FML Crenneville
Brigade Blumencron (five bns and eight guns)
Jäger Bn. Nr.4
IR Erzherzog Franz Karl Nr.52
Brigade Fehlmayer (five bns and eight guns)
Grenzinfanteriebataillon Titler
IR Erzherzog Ludwig Nr.8
Corps artillery (24 guns)
Corps cavalry, Ulanenregiment Nr.12 (four sqns)

XI KORPS – FML WEIGL
(12,486 infantry, 560 cavalry, 25 guns)
1.Division – FML Schwartzel
Brigade Sebottendorf* (five bns and eight guns)
Jäger Bn. Nr.10
IR Erzherzog Josef Nr.37
Brigade Greschke (four bns and eight guns)
IR Graf Khevenhüller Nr.35
2.Division – FML Blomberg
Brigade Baltin (five bns and eight guns)
Grenz IR Warasdiner-Creuzer Nr.5 Bn.2
IR Graf Hartmann-Klarstein Nr.9
Brigade Dobrzensky* (five bns and eight guns)
Jäger Bn. Nr.21
IR König von Hannover Nr.42
Brigade Host* (five bns and eight guns)
Grenz IR Nr.9 Peterwardeiner Bn.2
IR Grossherzog von Mecklenburg-
Schwerin Nr.57
Corps artillery (eight guns)
Corps cavalry, Ulanenregiment Nr.4 (four sqns)

KAVALLERIEDIVISION – FML ZEDTWITZ
(2,970 cavalry, 16 guns)
Brigade Vopaterny (16 sqns and eight guns)
Husarenregiment Nr.3
Husarenregiment Nr.11
Brigade Lauingen (12 sqns and eight guns)
Dragonerregiment Nr.1
Dragonerregiment Nr.3
Army artillery reserve (24 guns, 16 used)

Zweite Armee – FZM Graf Schlick

I KORPS – FML GRAF EDOUARD CLAM GALLAS
(15,190 infantry, 480 cavalry, 56 guns)
1.Division – FML Montenuovo
Brigade Paszthory (five bns and eight guns)
Jäger Bn. Nr.2*
IR Prinz Wasa Nr.60
Brigade Brunner (six bns and eight guns)
Grenz IR 2.Banal Nr.11 Bn.1 and 2
IR Graf Thun-Hohenstein Nr.29
2.Division – FML Stankoviç
Brigade Hoditz (five bns and eight guns)
Jäger Bn. Nr.14
IR Erzherzog Ernst Nr.48
Brigade Reczniçek (five bns and eight guns)
Jäger Bn. Nr.24
IR Baron Wernhardt Nr.16

Corps artillery (24 guns)
Corps cavalry, Husarenregiment Nr.12 (four sqns)

V KORPS – FML GRAF STADION
(19,596 infantry, 480 cavalry, 60 guns)
1.Division – FML Palffy
Brigade Gaal (five bns and eight guns)
Grenz IR Liccaner Nr.1 Bn.1
IR Erzherzog Karl Nr.3
Brigade Puchner (five bns and eight guns)
Kaiserjäger Bn. Nr.4
IR Baron Culoz Nr.31
Brigade Bils (five bns and eight guns)
Grenz IR Oguliner Nr.3 Bn.2
IR Graf Kinsky Nr.47
2.Division – FML Sternberg
Brigade Koller (five bns and eight guns)
Grenz IR Oguliner Nr.3 Bn.1
IR Herzog von Modena Nr.32
Brigade Festetics (five bns and eight guns)
Kaiserjäger Bn. Nr.6
IR Baron Reischach Nr.21
Corps artillery (20 guns)
Corps cavalry, Ulanenregiment Nr.12 (four sqns)

VII KORPS – FML BARON ZOBEL
(15,728 infantry, 480 cavalry, 32 guns)
1.Division – FML Prinz von Hesse
Brigade Wussin (five bns and eight guns)
Grenz IR Liccaner Nr.1 Bn.2
IR Kaiser Franz Josef Nr.1
Brigade Gablenz (six bns and eight guns)
Kaiserjäger Bn. Nr.2
Grenz IR Szluiner Nr.4 Bn.1
IR Baron Grüber Nr.54
2.Division – FML Lilia
Brigade Brandenstein (five bns and eight guns)
Jäger Bn. Nr.19
IR Erzherzog Luitpold Nr.53
Brigade Wallon (five bns and eight guns)
Grenz IR Otocaner Nr.2 Bn.1
IR Graf Wimpffen Nr.22
Corps artillery (16 guns)*
Corps cavalry, Husarenregiment Nr.1 (four sqns)

VIII KORPS – FML GRAF BENEDEK
(20,160 infantry, 560 cavalry, 72 guns)
1.Division – FML Berger
Brigade Watervliet (five bns and eight guns)
Kaiserjäger Bn. Nr.2
IR Baron Prohaska Nr.7
Brigade Kuhn (five bns and eight guns)
Grenz IR Szluiner Nr.4 Bn.2
IR Kronprinz Albert von Sachsen Nr.11
2.Division – FML Lang
Brigade Philipoviç (five bns and eight guns)
Kaiserjäger Bn. Nr.5
IR Prinz Hohenlohe-Langenburg Nr.17
Brigade Dauber (five bns and eight guns)
Jäger Bn. Nr.3
IR Dom Miguel Nr.39
Brigade Lippert (five bns and eight guns)

Jäger Bn. Nr.9

IR Erzherzog Rainer Nr.59

Brigade Reichlin (from VI Korps 22 June)

(four bns and eight guns)

4th Bns: IR Nr.9, 18, 19, 27

Corps artillery (24 guns)

Corps cavalry, Husarenregiment Nr.1 (four sqns)

KAVALLERIEDIVISION – FML MENSDORFF

(2,600 cavalry, 16 guns)

Brigade Holstein (12 sqns and eight guns)

Dragonerregiment Nr.5

Dragonerregiment Nr.6

Brigade Zichy (eight sqns and eight guns)

Ulanenregiment Nr.1

Army artillery reserve (112 guns)*

FRENCH ARMY, 24 JUNE 1859

Corps and division commanders were *généraux de division*, unless shown as *maréchaux*; Brigade commanders were *généraux de brigade*. Both formations were known by their commander's surname. The names of previous commanders, killed or promoted since the start of the campaign, appear in parentheses.

French battalions had six companies of about 100 men each; cavalry regiments four squadrons averaging 130 men each. Most infantry regiments had three battalions, except the *zouaves* of the Guard and 1er Régiment étranger (Foreign Legion). *Chasseurs à pied* or light infantry operated as single battalions.

Artillery batteries had six guns, generally rifled *pièces de quatre* firing 4kg shells, i.e. 9-pdrs in British terminology. Infantry divisions had two field batteries, where the gunners rode on the limbers, and a company of engineers. Cavalry had one or two horse batteries where the gunners rode separately. Corps artillery reserves had a mixture of field, horse and foot batteries. The latter had *pièces de douze* firing 12kg shells (26-pdrs). The tables specify types for reserve batteries.

Numbers engaged by each corps at Solferino are shown in parentheses. Divisional totals are also given, whether engaged or not. Numbers differed slightly from Magenta, newly arrived reservists replacing casualties.

NB: * Not present at Solferino

Commander-in-chief – His Imperial Highness Napoleon III

Chief of staff – Maréchal Vaillant

GARDE IMPÉRIALE – MARÉCHAL REGNAUD DE ST JEAN D'ANGÉLY (PROMOTED AFTER MAGENTA)

(14,022 infantry, 3,259 cavalry, 36 guns)

1er Division – Mellinet

(6,313 infantry and 12 foot guns)

Brigade Niol (ex-Cler) (five bns)

Zouaves

1er Grenadiers

Brigade Blanchard (ex-de Wimpffen) (six bns)

2e Grenadiers

3e Grenadiers

2e Division – Camou

(7,709 infantry and 12 horse guns)

Brigade Manèque (seven bns)

Chasseurs à pied

1er Voltigeurs

2e Voltigeurs

Brigade Picard (ex-Decaen) (six bns)

3e Voltigeurs

4e Voltigeurs

Division de cavalerie – Morris

(3,259 cavalry and 12 guns)

Brigade Marion (eight sqns)

1er Cuirassiers

2e Cuirassiers

Brigade de Champeron (eight sqns)

Dragons

Lanciers

Brigade Cassaignolles (eight sqns)

Chasseurs à cheval

Guides

Corps artillery (one field and one foot bty, 12 guns)*

I CORPS – MARÉCHAL BARAGUEY D'HILLIERS

(20,527 infantry, 2,457 cavalry, 66 guns)

1er Division – Forey

(6,602 infantry and 12 guns)

Brigade Dieu (ex-Beuret) (seven bns)

17e Chasseurs à pied

74e Ligne

84e Ligne

Brigade d'Alton (ex-Blanchard) (six bns)

91e Ligne

98e Ligne

2e Division – Ladmirault

(6,968 infantry and 12 guns)

Brigade Félix Douay (ex-Niol) (seven bns)

10e Chasseurs à pied

15e Ligne

21e Ligne

Brigade de Négrier (six bns)

61e Ligne

100e Ligne

3e Division – Bazaine

(8,307 infantry and 12 guns)

Brigade Goze (nine bns)

1er Zouaves

33e Ligne

34e Ligne

Brigade Dumont (six bns)

37e Ligne

78e Ligne

Division de cavalerie – Desvaux

(2,457 cavalry and six guns)

Brigade de Planhol (eight sqns)

5e Hussards

1er Chasseurs d'Afrique

Brigade de Forton (eight sqns)

2e Chasseurs d'Afrique

3e Chasseurs d'Afrique

Corps artillery (two field, one horse and one foot bty, 24 guns)

II CORPS – MARÉCHAL DE MACMAHON (PROMOTED AFTER MAGENTA)

(16,156 infantry, 1,347 cavalry, 48 guns)

1er Division – La Motterouge

(7,902 infantry and 12 guns)

Brigade Lefèbvre (six bns)

Tirailleurs Algériens

45e Ligne

Brigade Abel Douay (ex-de Polhès) (six bns)

65e Ligne

70e Ligne

2e Division – Decaen (ex-Espinasse)

(8,254 infantry and 12 guns)

Brigade Gault (seven bns)

11e Chasseurs à pied

71e Ligne

72e Ligne

Brigade de Castagny (eight bns)

2e Zouaves

1er Régiment étranger

2e Régiment étranger

Brigade de cavalerie – Gaudin de Vilaine

(1,347 cavalry) (eight sqns)

4e Chasseurs à cheval

7e Chasseurs à cheval

Corps artillery (two field, one horse and one foot bty, 24 guns)

III CORPS – MARÉCHAL CANROBERT

(11,204 infantry, 1,113 cavalry, 24 guns)

1er Division – Renault

(8,070 infantry and 12 guns)

Brigade Doëns (ex-Picard) (seven bns)

8e Chasseurs à pied

23e Ligne

90e Ligne

Brigade Jannin (six bns)

41e Ligne

56e Ligne

2e Division – Trochu

(7,067 infantry and 12 guns)

Brigade Bataille (seven bns)

19e Chasseurs à pied

43e Ligne

44e Ligne

Brigade Collineau (six bns)*

64e Ligne

88e Ligne

3e Division – Bourbaki

(7,876 infantry and 12 guns)*

Brigade Vergé (seven bns)

18e Chasseurs à pied

11e Ligne

14e Ligne

Brigade Ducrot (six bns)

46e Ligne

59e Ligne

Division de cavalerie – Partouneaux

(1,113 cavalry and six guns)

Brigade de Clérambault (eight sqns)

2e Hussards

7e Hussards

Brigade de Labareyre (eight sqns)

1er Lanciers

4e Lanciers

Corps artillery (two field, two horse and one foot bty, 30 guns)*

IV CORPS – GÉNÉRAL NIEL

(21,026 infantry, 986 cavalry, 66 guns)

1er Division – de Luzy de Pelissac

(7,864 infantry and 12 guns)

Brigade C. Douay (seven bns)

5e Chasseurs à pied

30e Ligne

49e Ligne

Brigade Lenoble (six bns)

6e Ligne

8e Ligne

2e Division – Vinoy

(6,045 infantry and 12 guns)

Brigade de Capriol (ex-Martimprey) (seven bns)

6e Chasseurs à pied

52e Ligne

73e Ligne

Brigade de la Charrière (six bns)

85e Ligne

86e Ligne

3e Division – de Failly

(7,117 infantry and 12 guns)

Brigade O'Farrell (seven bns)

15e Chasseurs à pied

2e Ligne

53e Ligne

Brigade Saurin (six bns)

55e Ligne

76e Ligne

Brigade de cavalerie – de Rochefort

(986 cavalry) (eight sqns)

2e Chasseurs à cheval

10e Chasseurs à cheval

Corps artillery (two field, two horse and one foot bty, 30 guns)

V CORPS – PRINCE NAPOLEON*

1er Division – d'Autemarre

(12,112 infantry and 12 guns)

Brigade Neigre (nine bns)

3e Zouaves

75e Ligne

89e Ligne

Brigade Corréard (six bns)

93e Ligne

99e Ligne

2e Division – Uhrich

(8,948 infantry and 12 guns)

Brigade Grandchamp (seven bns)

14e Chasseurs à pied

18e Ligne

26e Ligne

Brigade du Bourguet (six bns)

80e Ligne

82e Ligne

Brigade de cavalerie – de Lapérouse

(1,044 cavalry and six guns) (eight sqns)

6e Hussards

8e Hussards

Corps artillery – not arrived in theatre

SARDINIAN ARMY, 24 JUNE 1859

Sardinian regiments had four battalions of four companies with an establishment of 150 bayonets each. Cavalry regiments fielded four squadrons of 100 sabres, against an establishment of 145. Sardinian light batteries had four SB 8-pdr bronze guns and two 15cm howitzers; heavy batteries had eight 16-pdr guns. Infantry divisions had two light batteries and one heavy; the cavalry reserve two light batteries with additional horses. There were also six reserve batteries of 16-pdrs or howitzers that did not see action. Weapon designations did not accurately reflect projectile weights:

Piece	Projectile	Case shot
8-pdr	3kg ball	5.22kg
16-pdr	6kg ball	10.2kg
15cm	8kg shell	12kg

Most brigades were territorial, named after the area where they were raised. They were commanded by a *maggior generale*, whose names follow their unit's title.

NB: Throughout the campaign the light cavalry were distributed as required, operating with both Sardinian and French formations. Regiments rarely served with their parent division as complete units.

* Not present at Solferino

Commander-in-chief – King Vittorio Emmanuele

Ad Latus – Generale Alfonso La Marmora

Chief of staff – Luogotenente Generale della Rocca

1ª Divisione – Luogotenente Generale Giovanni Durando (ex-Castelborgo)

(9,034 infantry, 410 cavalry, 20 guns)

Brigata Granatieri – Scozia di Galliano (nine bns)

3° Battiglione Bersaglieri

1° Reggimento Granatieri

2° Reggimento Granatieri

Brigata Savoia – Perrier

4° Battiglione Bersaglieri

1° Reggimento di Fanteria

2° Reggimento di Fanteria

Reggimento Cavallegeri di 'Alessandria' (four sqns)

2ª Divisione – Luogotenente Generale Manfredo Fanti

(9,629 infantry, 351 cavalry, 20 guns)

Brigata Piemonte – Camerana (nine bns)

9° Battiglione Bersaglieri

3° Reggimento di Fanteria

4° Reggimento di Fanteria

Brigata Aosta – Cerale (nine bns)

1° Battiglione Bersaglieri

5° Reggimento di Fanteria

6° Reggimento di Fanteria

Reggimento Cavallegeri di 'Aosta' (four sqns)

3ª Divisione – Luogotenente Generale Filiberto Mollard (ex-Durando)

(8,999 infantry, 389 cavalry, 20 guns)

Brigata Cuneo – Arnaldi (nine bns)

10° Battiglione Bersaglieri

7° Reggimento di Fanteria

8° Reggimento di Fanteria

Brigata Pinerolo – Morozzo della Rocca (nine bns)

2° Battiglione Bersaglieri

13° Reggimento di Fanteria

14° Reggimento di Fanteria

Reggimento Cavallegeri di 'Montferrato' (four sqns)

4ª Divisione – Luogotenente Generale Enrico Cialdini*

Brigata Regina – Villamarina (nine bns)

7° Battiglione Bersaglieri

9° Reggimento di Fanteria

10° Reggimento di Fanteria

Brigata Savona – Broglia (nine bns)

6° Battiglione Bersaglieri

15° Reggimento di Fanteria

16° Reggimento di Fanteria

Reggimento Cavallegeri di 'Novara' (four sqns)

5ª Divisione – Luogotenente Generale Domenico Cucchiari

(9,512 infantry, 412 cavalry, 20 guns)

Brigata Casale – Genova di Pettinengo nine bns)

8° Battiglione Bersaglieri

11° Reggimento di Fanteria

12° Reggimento di Fanteria

Brigata Acqui – Gozani di Treville (nine bns)

5° Battiglione Bersaglieri

17° Reggimento di Fanteria

18° Reggimento di Fanteria

Reggimento Cavallegeri di 'Saluzzo' (four sqns)

Divisione di Cavalleria – Luogotenente Generale Sonnaz (ex-Sambuy)

(2,079 cavalry, 12 guns)

Reggimenti Cavallegeri di 'Nizza', 'Piemonte Reale', 'Savoia' and 'Genova'

OPPOSING PLANS

THE THEATRE OF WAR

The North Italian theatre of operations consists of a great river system. The river Po rises in the Alps, north and west of the Lombard plain, then flows south and then east towards the Adriatic. The northern spurs of the Apennines define the southern edge of what contemporaries called the strategic chessboard, closely approaching the right bank of the Po to form a strategic defile between Alessandria and Piacenza, opposing fortresses held by the Sardinians and Austrians respectively. A plain 144km long and 48km broad stretches along the Po's left bank, from the Sardinian capital at Turin to the Austrian fortresses of the Quadrilateral: Peschiera, Verona, Legnago and Mantua. The great river's tributaries flow southwards across this plain, forming a series of roughly parallel obstacles. The most significant of these in the 1859 campaign would be the Dora Baltea, Sesia, Ticino, Chiese and Mincio. The last formed the Quadrilateral's western edge between Peschiera and Mantua. These rivers are empty in summer, their wide gravelly beds filling up after rain, as the Sesia did during the action at Palestro. The Po was a major obstacle, 500m wide below its confluence with the Sesia at Valenza, with marshy banks.

'War in the Austrian fashion': French propaganda image of Austrian troops looting an Italian farmhouse. Habsburg logistics certainly left much to be desired, their troops dying from hunger and exhaustion during peacetime exercises. (Author/lemonde)

Austrian troops cross the river Po on a pontoon bridge. The great rivers of the North Italian plain shaped the campaign's strategic course. In the background are the Apennine mountains that enclosed the theatre of war to the south. (Author/Bossoli)

Otherwise the ground is flat and closely cultivated, much cut up with irrigation channels. West of the Ticino paddy-fields of rice predominate, making way for maize and wheat further east. Belts of trees and bushes line the streams, while everywhere fruit trees, laced with vines, presented serious obstacles to visibility and off road movement. Post roads were very good, metalled and running quite straight for kilometres. Country roads were mere tracks, becoming impassable in bad weather. Railways were usually single track. On the Piedmontese side they ran from Susa in the Alps via Turin to Vercelli and Novara, or to Alessandria, Voghera and Piacenza, as well as from Genoa via Novi to Alessandria, Valenza, Casale and Vercelli.

Austrian railways ran from Venice or the Tyrol through Verona, continuing westwards to Lake Como or Magenta on the river Ticino. Running at right angles to the front they could only serve as lines of communication. Some Piedmontese lines ran across the front, so could be used for tactical movements also.

The Quadrilateral formed the eastern edge of the theatre of war. It was not just a group of fortresses, but a vast entrenched battle ground, the value of which Radetzky had shown in 1848–49. Milan, however, lacked modern fortifications. It was bound to fall once the Allies established themselves east of the Ticino. The Piedmontese national redoubt of Alessandria served a similar purpose to the Quadrilateral. With its railways and fortified bridgehead at Casale, it formed a pivot around which the earlier part of the campaign would revolve.

AUSTRIAN PLANS

None of the three armies engaged in the Italian campaign conducted the war in accordance with any consistent strategic scheme or plan. The Austrians, who had precipitated the crisis, needed to launch an immediate offensive to achieve their political aim of humbling the Sardinian state. Radetzky had done just that in 1849. Gyulai, however, would have preferred to withdraw to the Austrian comfort zone of the Quadrilateral without a fight. This contradiction between the offensive requirements of Austria's foreign policy and her generals' defensive mindset persisted throughout the whole campaign. It went right to the top of the chain of command, Grünne and Hess competing daily for the Kaiser's ear. Compelled to invade Piedmont against his will, Gyulai fell between two stools, neither defeating the Sardinians before the French arrived, nor escaping to await reinforcements at a safe distance. His compromise strategy of passively defending the river lines in front of Milan left him open to an opportunistic attack by the more aggressive Allies. The debate between advocates of the offensive and defensive continued after several partial defeats compelled the Austrians to abandon Milan, and fall back across the river Mincio. In the end, the unresolved conflict between Grünne and Hess led to the disastrous decision to resume the offensive and recross the Mincio, bringing on the final battle at Solferino.

FRENCH PLANS

Napoleonic tradition demanded that strategy sprang fully formed from the genius of the emperor. Napoleon III, a born opportunist, seems to have had no strategy at all, beyond picking up a dynastically favourable success on the cheap. He depended on his wits to solve problems as they came along. When the Austrians retreated behind uncrossable water obstacles, he turned their flank, using the same rivers to protect his own flank. When the enemy abandoned Lombardy, the Allies simply followed at a distance, keeping well closed up to prevent hyperactive French corps commanders incurring unnecessary losses. When the Austrians counter-marched, the Allies fought them where they stood, trusting in the individual superiority of their soldiers to see them through. The result of Solferino suggests Napoleon III's calculations on that score were quite sound. He was also enough of a realist to seize the psychological moment and make peace, rather than batter his army to pieces against the Quadrilateral. He may not have been as great a strategist as his uncle, but he had a far keener sense of what was politically practicable.

French infantry sergeant wearing the simplified campaign dress in use at Solferino. The leather shako has made way for the kepi, soon to become standard headgear across the Atlantic. (Author/INW)

SARDINIAN PLANS

The Sardinians were the junior partner in the Franco-Italian alliance, but the first in the firing line. Their main concern, therefore, was to avoid annihilation in the weeks before sufficient French troops arrived to defeat or deter the Austrians. In the meantime, they pursued a classic defensive strategy, as recommended by Clausewitz, exploiting all the resources of their country – fortresses, obstacles (in this case rivers and inundations) and popular support – to postpone a decision and gain time for external factors (the intervention of an ally) to shift the balance of forces in their favour. It might not have worked against a more dynamic opponent, but did well enough against the half-hearted Austrians. After the war, Vittorio Emmanuele suggested a monument should be dedicated, not to himself, but to the Austrian commander-in-chief. Following the arrival of the French, the Sardinians cooperated loyally, acting as the left wing of the Allied army.

THE SOLFERINO CAMPAIGN

OPENING MOVES

The first serious event of the campaign was the Austrian passage of the Ticino into Piedmontese territory on 29 April with VII and V Korps at Bereguardo, III, VIII and II Korps at Pavia and the Reserve Division in the rear in order to keep order. Two more corps, XI and I under Schaafsgottsche and Clam Gallas respectively, had yet to arrive.

Gyulai's best plan was to crush the Sardinian Army, which he outnumbered two to one, before their allies arrived and shifted the odds against him. His advance, however, was slow and hesitant, only 32km in the first four days. It poured with rain. Roads disintegrated, rivers overflowed their banks and swept away bridges. Meanwhile, the Sardinians cut dykes and flooded the countryside. Vienna paralyzed Zweite Armee with contradictory telegrams: Grünne wanted Gyulai to stay behind the Ticino, Hess thought it better to retire on the Mincio, or defend the Chiese.

Gyulai's vacillations make his operations difficult to interpret, but they fall into three broad stages:

Sardinian sentry early in the war. Their campaign dress included greatcoats, even in summer. Note the low-lying, easily flooded, countryside in the background. (Author/ILN)

Austrian infantry embarking on Lake Maggiore at the northern end of the front line. Austria's strategic situation at the start of the war demanded swift and focussed action, not the aimless manoeuvres and detachments beloved of Habsburg generals. (Author/INW)

29 April to 8 May: he advanced on the Sardinian centre at Valenza and Casale, hampered by terrible weather. Benedek's VIII Korps crossed to the south bank of the Po, threatening Allied communications between Genoa and Alessandria, then retired without cutting the vital railway.

5–8 May: he ordered an advance by the right wing on Turin, which lay completely open except for a few cavalry and Garibaldi's irregulars.

9–10 May: he undertook a hurried retreat into the Lomellina, the low-lying area between the Sesia and Ticino, following reports of French forces at Alessandria, threatening the Austrian left flank.

Gyulai's actions are the more incomprehensible as his staff had produced a detailed study recommending the correct strategy. They recognized that the Sardinians would be without French support for a fortnight, and that Gyulai's proper objective was the Sardinian Army not Turin. An advance along both banks of the Po gave a good chance of a successful strike against the Sardinians, indefinitely postponing the junction of the widely separated French forces coming via Genoa and the Alpine passes. Such an advance would forestall an Allied riposte against the Austrian left, as it would stop up the mountain passes between Genoa and the Po valley. Instead, Gyulai wore out his troops to no purpose, marching up and down in the rain. Meanwhile the Allies concentrated their armies under Gyulai's nose, persuading him to withdraw from Piedmontese territory without a fight.

When the Austrians issued their ultimatum, neither Allied army was ready. The Sardinians were mobilized but scattered with 12,000 men in the defiles of the river Scrivia, securing the passes between Alessandria and Genoa, where their French allies would land. Another 32,000 men were spread over a 32km front between Casale and Alessandria. A large contingent of 20,000 was situated along the Dorea Baltea, further from their own headquarters than the Austrians were.

The French Army was still forming. Two routes, however, provided almost continuous steam communications between Paris and Alessandria. One was by rail to Toulon and Marseilles, then by sea to Genoa, and the other was by rail to the French side of the Alps at St Jean de Maurienne, and from Susa on the Piedmontese side.

Snow still blocked the 64km gap over the Alps, but 4,000 labourers were set to work clearing the road. Some Parisian regiments took only five days to

The Italian campaign: theatre of war and opening moves

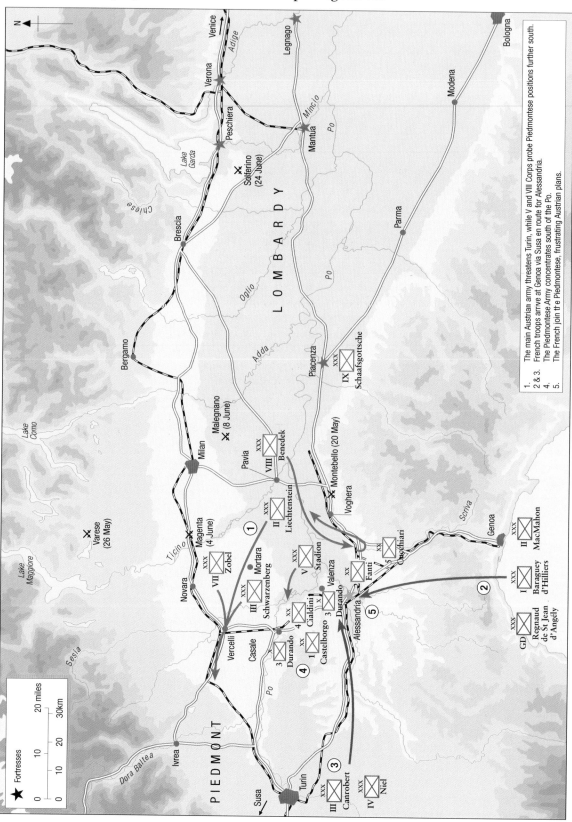

1. The main Austrian army threatens Turin, while V and VIII Corps probe Piedmontese positions further south.
2 & 3. French troops arrive at Genoa via Susa en route for Alessandria.
4. The Piedmontese Army concentrates south of the Po.
5. The French join the Piedmontese, frustrating Austrian plans.

ABOVE LEFT
French troops crossing the Mont Cenis pass between the French and Sardinian railheads at St Jean de Maurienne and Susa, respectively. Today the railway runs right through underneath the pass, through a tunnel. (Author/Bossoli)

BELOW LEFT
French steam auxiliary warships landing troops at Genoa. The rapid arrival of reinforcements from Algeria and Toulon pre-empted the dilatory Austrian offensive, and denied Graf Gyulai an easy victory over the smaller Sardinian Army. (Author/INW)

reach Alessandria, the sea passage from Toulon requiring just 24 hours, instead of the 20 marches needed previously. I and II corps (Baraguey and MacMahon) went by sea, the latter from Algeria, followed by the Guard (Regnaud) from Paris. Baraguey's leading elements landed in Genoa on 29 April, while the Austrians were still filing across the Ticino. III and IV corps (Canrobert and Niel) passed Susa on 29 April and 7 May respectively, concentrating at Alessandria by 9 May. The artillery and cavalry took longer, not arriving until the second fortnight in May. The Guard artillery only left Genoa on 15 May.

The French Army thus approached the theatre of operations in two separate wings. This might have proved embarrassing in face of a more active opponent. The Allied reaction to Gyulai's advance, however, was calculated to prevent him exploiting the gap between the French columns. The Sardinians had hoped to defend Turin directly on the Dora Baltea line. Maréchal Canrobert recommended a more circumspect strategy, concentrating the Sardinian Army in a flanking position at Alessandria to defend Turin indirectly. With French troops already at Genoa, the imminent appearance of red trousers on Gyulai's left flank would surely deter him from advancing on the capital. To Vittorio Emmanuele's incredulous relief, this proved to be the case.

OPPOSITE PAGE
The flood plain of the river Po is surrounded by mountains to north and south, and closed off to the east by the fortresses of the Quadrilateral: Verona, Peschiera, Mantua and Legnago. The Sardinian Army began the war at Alessandria, awaiting French reinforcements by rail via Turin, or by sea through Genoa. Meanwhile, the Austrians fumbled their invasion of Piedmont, the area between Turin and the river Sesia. The decisive battles of the war would be in Lombardy not Piedmont.

Panorama of Montebello from the high ground south of the battlefield, showing the village (centre) and low flat agricultural country beyond, stretching northwards towards the river Po. The Austrians approached from Casteggio on the right, the French along the poplar lined road from Voghera on the left. (Author/INW)

The opening crisis of the war was over by 12 May, when Napoleon III issued an order of the day evoking the cause of Italian liberation. He reminded his soldiers of French victories at Marengo and Rivoli, while exhorting them to maintain the severest discipline: 'Here, do not forget, there are no enemies except those who fight against you. In battle keep together, and do not leave your ranks to run forward. Avoid too high an elan; that is the only thing I fear.'

The new weapons, he suggested, were only dangerous at a distance. The bayonet would remain the terrible weapon of the French infantry.

Montebello: reconnaissance in force

Austrian fears for their left flank soon provided an opportunity to test this assumption. The Allied concentration at Alessandria convinced Gyulai that the enemy meant to advance between the river Po and the northern Apennines, turning his southern flank. On 19 May Graf Stadion of V Korps was sent to clear up the situation on the Po's right bank, with a reconnaissance in force. He formed three columns, and a reserve, displaying the traditional Austrian talent for frittering away their forces in unnecessary detachments:

On the left (moving along the main road to Casteggio from Stradella): FML Urban with two brigades under Schaafsgottsche and Braum: 6,769 infantry, 225 cavalry, 16 guns.

In the centre (moving by country roads through Casatisma and Robecco): FML Paumgarten with two brigades under Gaal and Bils: 9,946 infantry, 227 cavalry, 20 guns.

On the right (moving cross country to Oriolo): GM Prinz von Hessen with his own brigade: 5,158 infantry, 487 cavalry, 12 guns.

In reserve (north of Robecco): GM Boer with two battalions and the artillery reserve: 1,638 infantry, 225 cavalry, 20 guns.

Only some of these forces saw action: 18 battalions (18,708), three squadrons (600), and two batteries (16 guns). The troops came from four different formations, but Stadion further mixed them up, ensuring units and commanders were strangers to one another. The French assumed they had beaten full-strength regiments, and claimed afterwards to have fought 30,000 Austrians. German accounts halve that number.

Next day, Urban's column advanced quickly along the main road towards Voghera, driving off the Sardinian Guardia Nazionale at Casteggio, to reach Montebello by 1.30pm. Here he agreed with Stadion that he should occupy Genestrello, a hamlet one-and-a-half kilometres further on, before stopping for the day. The other columns made slow progress on the country roads to the north, although Brigade Gaal of Paumgarten's column was coming up. As yet there was little sign of the enemy.

The ground about to become the first battlefield of the war fell into two sectors. A continuous flat plain extended across the Austrian right: a patchwork of cornfields, vineyards and water meadows, cut up by ditches and embankments running down towards the Po. The railway and main road from Stradella to Voghera run across this area, about 900m apart, at the foot of the northern spurs of the Apennines, the mountains that formed the Austrian left. Montebello itself stood on one such spur: a single street of solidly built stone houses at right angles to the main road. At the north end of the village, near the main road, was the cemetery, with its characteristic high stone wall and iron gate. Dirt tracks ran down from Montebello to Genestrello, which stood on a lower spur, dominating the open country as far as the Staffora River to the west.

Stadion was astonished to hear heavy firing from Genestrello at about 2.30pm. Urban's leading troops had suddenly run into aggressive infantry from Général Forey's division of I Corps (Baraguey). The French had been expecting an Austrian attack. 'Remember', Forey told his men, 'that your fathers always beat this enemy, and you will do as they did.' When Piedmontese church bells rang the alarm, Forey strengthened his outposts to four battalions. For a while they had to fight desperately. Austrian reinforcements pressed forward along the road and railway line despite repeated charges by the Sardinian Novara and Montferrato light cavalry regiments, which forced them to form square, but the arrival of Forey's main body stabilized the situation. In the plain, Brigade Blanchard occupied the farmhouse strongpoint of Cascina Nuova on a stream known as the Fossa Gazza, while Brigade Beuret took the high ground on the French right. Stadion outnumbered Forey three to one, but the latter's concentration at the decisive point before Montebello gave the French local numerical superiority. They deployed as follows:

Five battalions at Cascina Nuova against two from Brigade Braum (3,000 vs. 2,000).

Six battalions at Genestrello against three of Brigade Schaafsgottsche (3,600 vs. 2,400).

Meanwhile Hesse was held in check between Casatisma and Oriolo by the Aosta light cavalry regiment and a couple of battalions, which he

French infantry and Sardinian lancers of the Novara and Montferrato light cavalry regiments drive the Austrians back up the main road past Genestrello, towards Montebello silhouetted on the hillside above. (Author/INW)

The action at Montebello, 20 May (up to 4.30pm)

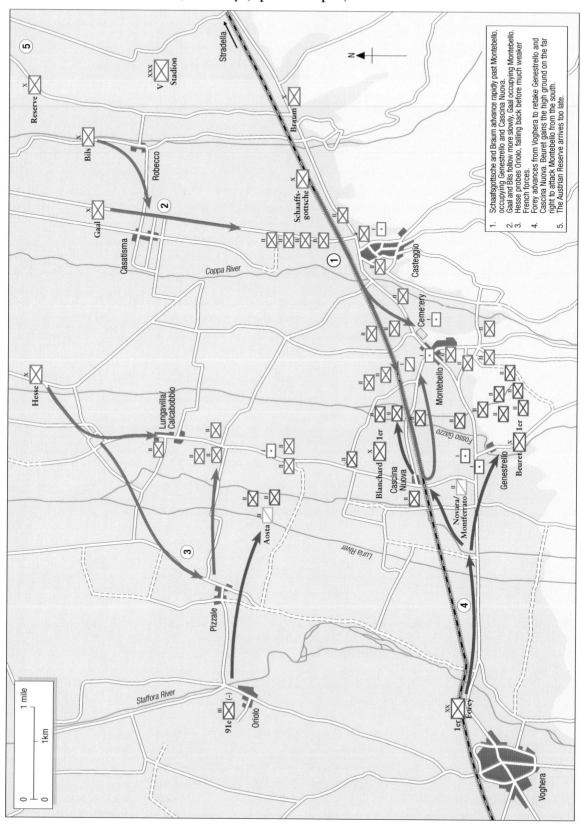

1. Schaafsgottsche and Braum advance rapidly past Montebello, occupying Genestrello and Cascina Nuova.
2. Gaal and Bils follow more slowly. Gaal occupying Montebello.
3. Hesse probes Oriolo, falling back before much weaker French forces.
4. Forey advances from Voghera to retake Genestrello and Cascina Nuova. Beuret gains the high ground on the far right to attack Montebello from the south.
5. The Austrian Reserve arrives too late.

outnumbered three to one. By 3pm the Austrians had lost Genestrello, forcing Braum's men to fall back also. Reinforced by three battalions of Brigade Gaal, Schaafsgottsche's men barricaded the village. Forey resumed his attack between 4 and 5pm with ten battalions (6,000 men). Blanchard menaced Montebello from below, while Beuret continued his right flanking movement on the high ground. Forey had lost his numerical edge, but Montebello's defenders were shaken by their previous rough handling.

Leaving his horse, Forey joined the skirmish line like the old *chasseur* that he was. Tall wheat hid Austrian *Jäger*, fresh enemy springing out of the earth at every step the French took. Reaching the outskirts of the village, the attackers paused to reload, before winkling out the defenders one house at a time. At length only the cemetery remained in Austrian hands, spitting fire like a volcano. Beuret was shot dead, but his men resolutely stormed the improvised redoubt. The only Austrians left in Montebello by 6.30pm were either dead or prisoners. Forey brought up his guns to consolidate the position, but did not pursue.

The Austrian high command were strangely pleased with their defeat. They believed Stadion had met the whole of Baraguey's I Corps, a battalion of Bazaine's Division having joined in without orders. This exaggerated estimate of French numbers confirmed Gyulai's fears for his left flank. However, he had lost over 1,300 men to find out what he might have learned from the newspapers. Austrian losses, including officers, were 331 killed, 785 wounded and 307 missing. The French admitted 105 killed, 549 wounded and 69 missing. Montebello starkly revealed the contrasting military style of the combatants. The Austrians took such pains to secure their retreat by leaving detachments along their line of advance that only half their force was engaged. The reserve arrived just in time to cover the retreat. Forey, by contrast, attacked with every available battalion. He had also set a fashion for the bayonet that would persist throughout the campaign.

THE ALLIED OFFENSIVE

The day after Montebello, Garibaldi crossed the river Sesia at Romagnano, well north of the Austrian right. Skirting the southern shore of Lake Maggiore, he pushed on to Varese, local volunteers swelling his original

French and Austrian infantry (right and left respectively) fight it out on the slopes below Montebello, as Forey's flanking movement takes effect. The *général* is on the right, having just dismounted. (Author/ILN)

3,120 *cacciatori* to 6,000. Gyulai dismissed Garibaldi's intrusion as an obvious diversion. FML Urban, responsible for rear area security, hurried north with one brigade, attacking Varese on 26 May with 3,000 men. He was defeated there and at San Fermo near Como, and chased all the way back to Monza, on the north-east outskirts of Milan. Reinforced by two more brigades, Urban retook Varese on 29 May, while Garibaldi was away raising the country. Garibaldi retreated on Laveno, hoping to escape across Lake Maggiore. Repulsed by the Austrian garrison there, he was trapped between the lakes and neutral Swiss territory. However, before Urban could catch him, Garibaldi was saved by a dramatic change in the strategic situation.

Garibaldi's expedition was part of a pattern of Allied activity that began soon after the Austrians had evacuated Vercelli on 19 May. Sardinian infantry crossed the river Sesia, and reoccupied some islands opposite Candia, until persuaded to withdraw by a vigorous response from Zobel's VII Korps and rising floodwaters, following five days of rain. These minor operations provided a convincing demonstration of the hopelessness of river crossings in face of an alert enemy. They confirmed Napoleon III in his personal preference for a bloodless solution to the problem of evicting Gyulai from the Lomellina and liberating Milan. There were three ways the Allies could achieve this. Firstly, through a right flanking move along the south bank of the Po. The Allies would have to advance down a single road hemmed in between the river and the Apennines, only to find the Austrian-held fortress of Piacenza blocking the eastern exit. Meanwhile, the Allied left flank would be exposed to attack by Austrian forces north of the Po in the Lomellina, waiting to counter just such a move.

Garibaldi's volunteers in action at San Fermo near Como. The Cacciatori delle Alpi were deployed in the mountains on the Allies' extreme left, the most appropriate area for guerrillas. (Author/Bossoli)

The local population cheer a column of Sardinian heavy cavalry and transport as it crosses the river Sesia at Cerreto, during the great Allied counter-march across the Austrian front. (Author/INW)

Secondly, through a frontal advance over the lower Sesia from Valenza or Casale, across a patchwork of rice fields, into the heart of the enemy's prepared defences. Even if such an advance suceeded, it would achieve little, as the Austrians could retire behind the Ticino, leaving the Allies no better off than before.

Thirdly, a left flanking manoeuvre around Gyulai's over-extended right flank, across the readily fordable reaches of the upper Sesia. Once at Novara the Allies would be nearer Milan, the ill-fortified and politically inflammable capital of Lombardy, than many Austrian units.

The only practical option was the third one. Traditionally a flank march directly across the enemy's front ran the risk of being attacked in flank itself. Such an outcome in this case was unlikely. Gyulai's attention was clearly focussed south of the Po. The rivers flowing across the Austrian front were impenetrable barriers to reconnaissance and counter-offensive alike. Just to be sure, the Allies mounted elaborate deception arrangements. I and II corps (Baraguey and MacMahon) massed threateningly at Voghera, on the Allied right. Bridges were prepared over the Po, guarded by the *Légion étrangère*, and masses of wagons were collected at Alessandria.

The key factor in the success of the manoeuvre was the 96km of railway from Voghera to Vercelli. Previously such a distance would have required four or five days solid marching. Baraguey's Corps would make the trip by train in a single day. The real danger of the strategy, apart from burst locomotive boilers, was that any defeat after the change of front might force the Allied army to retreat into neutral Switzerland, where they would face internment. Napoleon III, however, could trust his army and outnumbered the enemy. Acting with energy he could expect to throw the Austrians off balance, forcing them either to retreat and lose Milan, or to fight in a position not of their choosing. Compelled to face north instead of west, they too would face the prospect of being driven off their lines of communications, back into the bend of the Po.

A final conference at Vercelli on 26 May agreed the orders. The Sardinians had a key role, attacking the Austrian right between Vercelli and Mortara in order to screen the northwards movement of the French Army, across the Sardinian rear. Trestle bridges appeared over the Sesia at Vercelli on the 27th, the Allied armies moving north on the 28th. By 29 May all five Sardinian divisions (over 50,000 men) were at Vercelli closely supported by the French

Guard, III and IV corps at Casale (another 60,000). MacMahon's II Corps was at Valenza, while I Corps (Baraguey) brought up the rear at Sale and Bassignana. Allied headquarters remained at Alessandria as a deception measure. Gyulai regarded the Sardinian moves as a hoax, though his outposts plainly heard the locomotives whistling beyond the river.

The Allied Army moved like a giant snake to avoid becoming over-extended, pulling up its tail before pushing its head forward again. The French corps moved in reverse numerical order, led by Général Adolphe Niel's IV Corps, sleeping every night in the campsites left by their predecessors. Niel reached Novara on 1 June, to be greeted by jubilant, flag-waving crowds. Napoleon had placed 90,000 men across the Austrian flank without any interruption from the enemy. Contemporary critics compared the Allied flank march with the first Napoleon's more famous manoeuvres for its clearness of design, forethought of detail and well-ordered accuracy of execution. Although less immediate in its results, its broad strategic sweep bore comparison with the 1805 manoeuvre upon Ulm. Meanwhile the Sardinians' covering mission brought them two days' fighting at Palestro.

The action at Palestro: 30–31 May

The Sardinian soldiers received their orders to cross the Sesia with enthusiasm. They advanced on a three-division front about five kilometres across, wheeling on their right flank to face south-east, as follows:

2ª (Fanti)	via Borgo Vercelli and Casalino to Confienza.
3ª (Durando)	via Torrione to Vinzaglio.
4ª (Cialdini)	straight down the Mortara road to Palestro.
1ª (Castelborgo)	in reserve behind Fanti.

Feld-Marschall-Leutnant Baron Zobel's VII Austrian Korps held Palestro and Vinzaglio with outposts drawn from Lilia's Division, about a battalion all told. No doubt Lilia hoped to reinforce these detachments from Robbio, but they were taken by surprise, despite the Sardinians' slow advance along narrow tracks across flooded rice fields. All the country is very flat, but broken and criss-crossed with irrigation ditches. The villages stood on slight rises, surrounded by canals lined with tall grass, willow trees and poplars. Cialdini and Durando advanced under similar circumstances, with the main body on the embankments, screened by *bersaglieri* on either flank, supported by a lively shellfire at 1,350m. The defenders had loopholed the houses and entangled the narrow bridges with cut-down trees, covered by artillery, but the Sardinians had a great numerical advantage. They drove in the Austrian skirmishers, forced the barricades and bayoneted the gunners. Supporting Austrian battalions appeared during the fighting, but were too few to change the result. Palestro was in Sardinian hands by 4.30pm, Vinzaglio by 6.30pm. The misguided obstinacy of an Austrian battalion at Palestro cost them 560 casualties, including 284 prisoners.

Overnight the local peasantry helped barricade their villages, while the French moved III Corps (Canrobert) down to the Sesia at Prarolo to provide support next day. Unfortunately the river rose almost a metre after another day's solid rain, new channels appearing where previously only hollows had been visible. Despite the engineers' efforts, the only French troops directly supporting Cialdini next morning were 2,600 men of 3e Zouaves, sent round via Vercelli to cover the bridging operations. Strictly the regiment belonged to d'Autemarre's division of V Corps (Prince Napoleon), but it had transferred temporarily to Canrobert's Corps for the current operations.

Next day, Zobel tried to retake his lost outposts. As his other division was watching the lower Sesia, he reinforced Lilia with Jellaçic's Division from II Corps (Liechtenstein). The brigades fanned out from Robbio at 8.30am from right to left, as follows:

Brigade and Objective	Men
Weigl to Confienza	2,600
Dondorf to Palestro by the post road	3,500
Szabo south of Palestro via Rivoltella	3,900
Kudelka behind Dondorf in reserve	3,900
TOTAL	13,900

Since all three leading Sardinian divisions were now in line, Zobel was outnumbered two-to-one, without counting any other Allied troops.

The Austrian columns came into action about 10am. Fanti's 2^a Division outnumbered Weigl by at least four to one, so the Austrians' right flanking column made no progress at all. The main attack at Palestro did better against Cialdini's 4^a Division. While the Sardinian Brigata Regina held up Dondorf east of the village, Szabo turned Cialdini's right flank, by advancing along the riverbank, and brought Canrobert's pontoon bridge at Prarolo under artillery fire. Soon, however, Szabo's own troops came under enfilading fire from two French batteries (12 guns) beyond the Sesia. Worse was to follow. The Austrian advance had taken them across the front of 3e Zouaves, screened by poplar trees along the Sesietta, an arm of the Sesia. The *zouaves* formed regimental assault formation, two battalions up and one back in reserve. The two leading battalions deployed two companies each in skirmish order, supported by two columns of four companies each. The six companies of the third battalion remained in column. Wading through waist-deep water without firing a shot, 3e Zouaves overran Szabo's battery, and erupted into the left rear of Jäger Bn. Nr.7, already at grips with Cialdini's Brigata Savona behind Palestro. Szabo lost all his eight guns, and the *Jäger* were driven back upon the rest of the brigade, who fled, being young soldiers unaccustomed to the Lorenz rifle. Unfortunately for the Austrians, the Allies reached the narrow bridge at Ponte Brida first, and 500 *Jäger* were drowned or captured, virtually annihilating the battalion.

Zobel realized the futility of further efforts between 2 and 3pm, withdrawing the centre column to Robbio. He had lost over 2,000 men, including 780 prisoners, compared with Allied losses of 600. On both days Austrian generals had uselessly committed their men against overwhelming numbers. The result of the actions at Palestro shows how little Gyulai realized the true state of affairs, or the progress of the vast movement around his right flank. He made no northwards move. Eleven Austrian divisions remained on the lower Sesia and Po, facing just four French.

The 3e Zouaves had suffered 46 killed, 229 wounded, and 20 missing, who had rolled into the canal. Vittorio Emmanuele had accompanied their headlong charge. Next day, in recognition of his courage, the regiment made the king an honorary corporal, diplomatically presenting him with some of the captured guns.

The Allied turning movement, 28 May–2 June

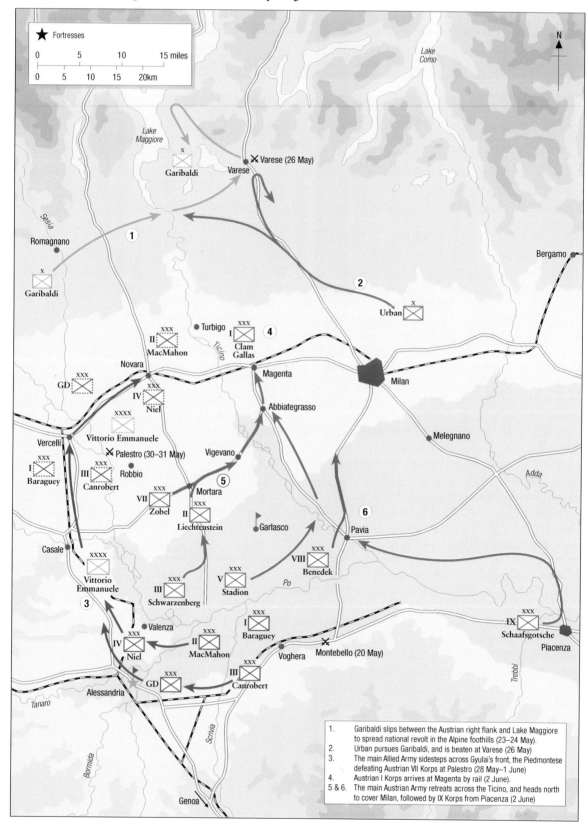

Fortresses

1. Garibaldi slips between the Austrian right flank and Lake Maggiore to spread national revolt in the Alpine foothills (23–24 May).
2. Urban pursues Garibaldi, and is beaten at Varese (26 May)
3. The main Allied Army sidesteps across Gyulai's front, the Piedmontese defeating Austrian VII Korps at Palestro (28 May–1 June)
4. Austrian I Korps arrives at Magenta by rail (2 June).
5 & 6. The main Austrian Army retreats across the Ticino, and heads north to cover Milan, followed by IX Korps from Piacenza (2 June)

Too little too late

The Allies' heavy deployment of seven divisions around Palestro was not unjustified. Gyulai's chief of staff, Oberst Kuhn, twice drafted orders for an advance by five corps into the flank of the Allied columns heading for Novara. Both times, however, Gyulai retired to bed with his tobacco pipe, and fell asleep with the orders still unsigned. His preference was an immediate retreat to the Mincio, to await reinforcements. The Austrians' eventual reaction to the Allied flank march was a compromise, retreating behind the Ticino to join I Korps (Clam Gallas). This was very much a half measure, as only two of Clam Gallas's four brigades had yet reached the railhead at Magenta, now only 19km east of the Allied advance guard at Novara.

The Austrian corps in the Lomellina began to pull back on 2 June in two groups, after numerous counter-orders and false starts. II (Liechtenstein), VII (Zobel) and III (Schwarzenberg) Korps moved from around Mortara to Vigevano on the Ticino. V (Stadion) and VIII (Benedek) Korps retreated from west of Pavia to Bereguardo on the Ticino.

The Naviglio Grande whose crossings became the strategic and tactical focus of the fighting at Magenta, photographed near Ponte Vecchio. The current is remarkable for a canal, enhancing its defensive potential. The trees on either bank appear much larger than in 1859. (Author/photo)

The retreat continued on 3 June with many delays, the troops tired and discouraged by the retirement. The second day's movements were as follows: II (Liechtenstein) from Vigevano northwards to Robecco and Magenta, VII (Zobel) to Abbiategrasso, III (Schwarzenberg) to Abbiategrasso. While V (Stadion) and VIII (Benedek) crossed at Bereguardo with the former heading for Abbiategrasso and the latter for Milan.

II and VII Korps became entangled, and only reached their bivouacs in the small hours. Feld-Marschall-Leutnant Hess caused more delay, arriving from Vienna for a crisis meeting with Gyulai. While the generals argued, the troops stood about uselessly for six hours, unable to cook their rations.

Meanwhile the French closed up to the Ticino. Camou's division of Guard *voltigeurs* arrived at Turbigo on 2 June, followed by II Corps (MacMahon) next day. The rest of the army concentrated around Novara, including the Sardinians who had completed their covering mission. Turbigo had no bridge, but it was unoccupied. A crossing there might give access to the east bank of the Naviglio Grande, a canal running alongside the Ticino as far as Abbiategrasso, south of Magenta, before turning eastwards for Milan. Camou's engineers worked all night to bridge the river by dawn on 3 June, covered by five batteries (30 guns).

This provided a double success. News of Camou's presence alarmed Clam Gallas, tasked with holding a bridgehead at San Martino, west of the Ticino. This was the pre-war Sardinian frontier post opposite Magenta, and should not be confused with San Martino della Battaglia, the Sardinian part of the Solferino battlefield. If Camou moved south he would cut off San Martino's defenders, so Clam Gallas pulled them back. Unfortunately his engineers' first attempt to blow up the main road bridge over the Ticino failed, and they had insufficient blasting powder for a second try. Only half the bridge collapsed, giving the Allies a second possible way for infantry to cross the Ticino. Many accounts refer to this bridge as the Ponte di Boffalora, which is correct, even though the village of Boffalora is three kilometres away to the north-east.

While the Austrians failed to seal off the bridges across the Ticino, MacMahon's II Corps crossed the pontoon bridge at Turbigo to consolidate Camou's bridgehead. MacMahon's troops were all from Algeria, including a newly raised regiment of native light infantry, or Tirailleurs Algériens.

Dressed in a similar Turkish style to *zouaves*, only in cornflower blue, these were known colloquially as 'Turcos'. In action for the first time as a regiment, the Tirailleurs pushed on to the village of Robecchetto, where they chased off an Austrian column belatedly exploring the country north of Magenta. Robechetto was in French hands by 2.30pm. MacMahon's three divisions bivouacked around Turbigo, ready to move southwards down the Ticino's left bank the following morning.

THE BATTLE OF MAGENTA

Neither side expected a battle on 4 June. Gyulai had ordered a day of rest. Napoleon III was justifiably surprised to find 40,000 Austrians holding the left bank of the Ticino so far north, after they had failed either to defend or destroy the river crossings. His scheme for the 4th was to consolidate his position astride the Ticino. MacMahon's II Corps would advance on Magenta with Camou's *voltigeurs* to join Mellinet's Division of Guard *grenadiers*, tasked with securing the bridges across the Naviglio Grande. Canrobert's III Corps would support Mellinet, his right flank covered by I and IV corps (Baraguey and Niel), who were echeloned back between Olengo and Trecate. Desvaux's and Partouneaux's cavalry divisions lay still further to the right rear. The Sardinians were to cross at Turbigo, moving across MacMahon's rear to cover his open left flank towards Milan.

As the battle developed unexpectedly, ostensible orders of battle had little to do with the forces actively engaged. On the Allied side these were:

	Infantry	Cavalry	Guns
LEFT WING			
II Corps (MacMahon)	17,766	1,097	39
Guard (Regnaud): Camou's Division	8,168		12
RIGHT WING			
Guard (Regnaud): Mellinet's Division	6,055	110	36
III Corps (Canrobert): Renault's and Trochu's divisions	11,041		
IV Corps (Niel): Vinoy's Division	6,915		
TOTALS	49,945	1,207	87

The Austrians failed to blow the main bridge over the river Ticino, allowing Allied troops to find a way across. Sardinian infantry follow the route taken by the Guard *grenadiers* on the morning of Magenta. (Author/Bossoli)

Two divisions of Sardinians and half of Canrobert's Corps never fired a shot, but they did provide some depth for the left and right flanks respectively. Austrian units engaged during the battle were as follows:

Initial location and formation	Infantry	Cavalry	Guns
MAGENTA			
I Korps (Clam Gallas)	10,767		24
II Korps (Liechtenstein)	15,612	519	48
ABBIATEGRASSO			
Reischach's Division of VII Corps (Zobel)	7,293	571	16
III Korps (Schwarzenberg)	20,391	1,145	56
CORBETTA			
Kavalleriedivision (Mensdorff)		1,200	
GARLASCO			
Brigade Dormus of V Korps (Stadion)	4,120		8
TOTALS	58,183	3,435	152

Zobel's other division (Lilia) marched up to Corbetta during the day, but remained in reserve. So did most of the army's reserve artillery.

The numbers given above are approximations. French accounts exaggerate the numbers of Austrians present, assuming they were at full strength, while ignoring their incomplete mobilization and high wastage rates on the march. The Austrians on the other hand had every reason to understate their strength after being beaten in such a strong position by markedly inferior numbers. Both armies were disproportionately strong on their left, and weak on their right. In the end, the collapse of the Austrian right at Magenta decided the day, while the French right wing held out by the narrowest of margins.

The Ticino has cut a wide bed through the Lombard plain, leaving broad level plateaux on either side. The river at Magenta flows nearer to the western plateau, which stands 12–21m above the riverbed. A low-lying area over a mile wide extends between the river and the eastern plateau. Densely covered with crops and fruit trees, it was partially flooded and difficult to traverse except along the road and railway embankments, which diverge once across

A general view of the Magenta battlefield, showing the Naviglio Grande running from Ponte Vecchio (foreground), past Ponte Nuovo and Boffalora, with the Alps in the background. (Author/Bossoli)

the Ticino. Beyond this area runs the swift-flowing Naviglio Grande, nine metres wide and two metres deep, its banks steep and overgrown with bushes. Maps gave little indication of how serious an obstacle this was, and Austrian outposts prevented Allied reconnaissance.

North of Boffalora, sometimes spelled Buffalora, the canal flows below the plateau's edge. Beyond that point it runs through a cutting that is only crossable at the bridges. The Austrians had mined the canal bridges at Boffalora and Ponte Vecchio, but not at Robecco five kilometres further south, where they might hope to use the bridge in a battle fought astride the canal. The new road and rail bridges at Ponte Nuovo had also been mined, but not yet blown. At the former stood four solid stone buildings, the pre-war customs post, occupying the angles formed by the road and canal. A redoubt secured the western end of the railway bridge, Austrian artillery sweeping its approaches from the eastern bank.

Three kilometres east of Ponte Nuovo stands the solidly built village of Magenta, commanding both the main road to Milan and the railway. North of Magenta lay the ground over which MacMahon would have to advance. It was level, studded with villages and farmhouses. Thorny acacia hedges enclosed densely cultivated fields, while rows of mulberry trees interlaced with vines hindered movement and blocked the view in every direction, even for a man on horseback.

The chambermaids of the Tuileries

Mellinet's Division of the Guard was weak, 11 battalions instead of the usual 13. It marched off from Trecate at 10am across an apparently deserted battlefield, although Général Mellinet could see suspicious movements beyond the canal. The guardsmen crossed the partly demolished bridge across the Ticino, manhandling across two guns, and leaving the divisional engineers to repair the roadway. For a while, their skirmishers exchanged long-range shots with Austrian outposts west of the Naviglio Grande, until Regnaud St Jean d'Angély, the corps commander, pulled them back to avoid pointless casualties. The emperor was waiting for MacMahon's expected advance. About 1.30pm, the rumble of cannon beyond Boffalora seemed to announce the guardsmen's opportunity. They resumed their advance in open columns of companies, spread out at full distance to reduce the risk of casualties from Austrian rockets that fell hissing in the flooded rice fields.

The commanders of the French corps most heavily engaged at Magenta: Patrice MacMahon of II Corps and Regnaud St Jean d'Angély of the Guard. Both were promoted to *maréchal* for their part in the victory. (Author/INW)

On the right 3e Grenadiers advanced to Ponte Vecchio across the fields, and Ponte Nuovo along the railway embankment. While in the centre: the Guard's two *zouave* battalions advanced to Ponte Nuovo, with 1er Grenadiers behind them in reserve. On the left 2e Grenadiers advanced to Boffalora by the country road.

The 3e Grenadiers took the western ends of the bridges quickly enough, but not before the retiring Austrians blew the Ponte Vecchio. The French had better luck at Ponte Nuovo, however. The *zouaves* passed through the leading *grenadiers* to storm the new road bridge, bayoneting an Austrian engineer about to fire the charges, and trundling several barrels of gunpowder into the canal. General-Major Burdina, the Austrian commander at Ponte Nuovo, was killed, while Brigade Szabo remembered their rough handling at Palestro and fled. The path appeared to be wide open for the Guard to march into Magenta and win the battle single-handed. The 2e Grenadiers on the left

The road bridge at Ponte Nuovo with modern pipework, and the western customs house on the left. The end wall of the house still shows signs of damage from shellfire. (Author/photo)

found Boffalora Bridge down already, but a quantity of planks lay carelessly about, which the *grenadiers* collected, awaiting their chance to place them across the shattered arches.

The heights beyond the canal were not yet in French hands, however. Staff officers craning their necks from a rooftop near the Ticino could see nothing of MacMahon's II Corps, while Canrobert's III Corps had yet to appear behind them at San Martino. So slow were the French supports in arriving that even Gyulai had time to react. He had received reports of the French approach as early as 8.15am, but did not appear at Magenta until 2pm. As news came in of the collapse at Ponte Nuovo, Gyulai ordered up Reischach's Division of VII Korps (Zobel) to restore the situation. Then he rode off to Robecco five kilometres in the rear, ostensibly to direct a counter-offensive against the French right flank with Schwarzenberg's III Korps. He did not return. A hostile newspaper reported that Gyulai had fled to Abbiategrasso after a shell burst over Robecco at maximum range. Whatever the truth, the promptness of Gyulai's departure from Magenta reinforces the bad impression created by his initial slowness to go forwards.

Reischach's counterattack succeeded brilliantly. Preceded by swarms of skirmishers, three battalions of Brigade Gablenz fell upon the *zouaves*' open flank, killing Général Cler, their brigade commander, and capturing one of the two field guns manhandled forward that morning. The other gun's detachment dragged it to safety, sabres in hand. The surviving infantry took refuge in the customs post by the bridge. Luckily for the French, Reischach was wounded, and Gablenz paused to collect his men before pressing his advantage. So dire was the French situation at 4pm, a single division of 5,000 worn-out soldiers opposed to an army, that Napoleon massed the Guard artillery on the steep west bank of the Ticino ready to cover a retreat. He himself stood poker-faced in the road behind Ponte Nuovo, for he had no other reserves to hand; every man of Mellinet's Division was in action except for the 1er Grenadiers' imperial security detachment of four companies. Meanwhile Gyulai was drafting telegrams to Franz Josef at Verona announcing an Austrian victory.

Brigade Kintzl of II Korps (Liechtenstein) opened Gyulai's counterstroke on the west bank of the canal at 4.30pm. Outnumbering 3e Grenadiers at Ponte Vecchio by 3,200 to 1,200 Kintzl drove them back to Ponte Nuovo, as far as

Densely cultivated countryside east of the Naviglio Grande. Small wheat fields alternate with maize, broken up with bushes and trees. This particular area, between Ponte Vecchio and Magenta, saw fierce fighting between Vinoy's Division and the Austrian IR Nr.27 (Author/photo)

the southern parapet of the Austrian entrenchment covering the bridge. Here the attack stalled as Brigade Picard of III Corps (Canrobert) arrived at the *pas de course* to greet the Austrians with a murderous fire. *Chasseurs* and *lignards* poured tumultuously over the earthworks, driving Kintzl's men back to Ponte Vecchio. Many of the Austrian troops were Italians and happy to surrender. The French soldiers on the other hand were delighted with their chance to rescue the guardsmen, known derisively as 'the chambermaids of the Tuileries', the palace where they were usually stationed. It was a piece of luck that a humble line regiment did not have every day.

Canrobert had been delayed by IV Corps (Niel) blocking the road through Novara, and did not reach Trecate until 2.30pm. Although fighting had been in progress for an hour Canrobert received no indication that he was desperately needed at the front, until his Piedmontese ADC arrived with an urgent appeal from the emperor. The effect was electric. Officers and men threw themselves in amongst the horses and baggage waggons that obstructed the road, and pressed on alone or in groups, reforming wherever the road allowed. Canrobert himself preceded his corps onto the battlefield to receive Napoleon's orders to take care of the right flank. He rode across the front to review the confused situation, sending one of his ADCs with 50 men to clear some Austrian snipers from a farmhouse. Dynamic leadership was in order. The Austrians still outnumbered the French heavily, as brigades Hartung and Dürfeld of III Korps (Schwarzenberg) moved up to replace Kintzl. Luckily for the French, the densely planted fruit trees concealed their numerical weakness. Picard shook out 8e Chasseurs and 23e Ligne into open order to harass the Austrian masses: 2,400 men against 8,000. His other regiment relieved the hard-pressed garrison of the customs post. Mellinet, who had lost two horses shot under him, could now gain a little depth by capturing a farm 540m beyond the canal. Three batteries of Guard artillery came up to consolidate the position around the canal bridges.

The French were still in difficulties. A last counterattack by Reischach drove the exhausted defenders of the bridgehead back to the canal bank again, but once more fresh troops tipped the balance in favour of the French. Vinoy's Division of IV Corps (Niel) arrived from Trecate at 5pm, deploying on a broad front to create the illusion of strength. At Ponte Nuovo his brigades divided: Martimprey pushed straight on up the main road towards

TOP RIGHT
One of the customs houses east of the canal, captured by the Guard *zouaves* at the start of the battle, and held against all odds. Today it stands beside a busy main road. (Author/photo)

BOTTOM RIGHT
The Austrian counterattack at Ponte Nuovo inflicted heavy losses on Brigade Cler, killing Général Cler, its commander. The square buildings in the background are the customs post. (Author/INW)

Magenta; de la Charrière turned right down the canal's left bank towards Ponte Vecchio. In confused fighting with Brigade Ramming of III Korps (Schwarzenberg) the village changed hands six times. French soldiers cut off beyond the canal called out to their comrades on the west bank to throw across fresh supplies of cartridges. After many delays, however, events on the battlefield's northern flank were about to turn the heroic efforts along the canal into victory.

The Duc de Magenta

MacMahon's II Corps and Camou's attached division of Guard *voltigeurs* moved off from the Turbigo bridgehead between 9.30 and 10.30am. La Motterouge's leading division approached Cuggione at midday, one-and-a-half kilometres short of the Austrian outposts at Casate, but Espinasse's Division took a more circuitous route via Castano to Marcallo on the army's extreme left wing. Close terrain confined movement to the roads, with lengthy halts to

The battle of Magenta, 4 June (early afternoon)

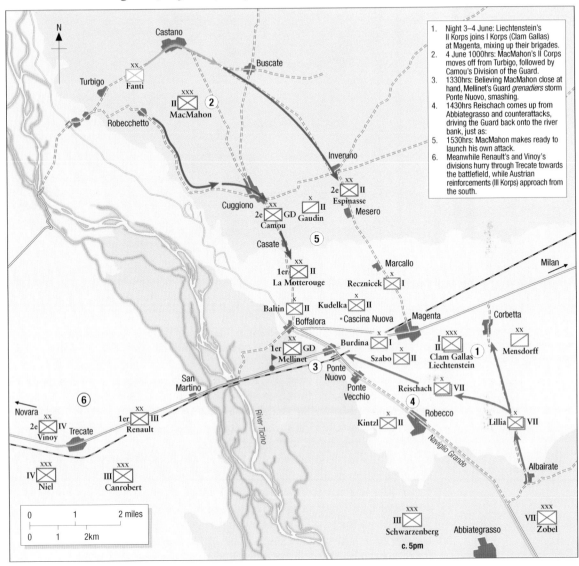

1. Night 3–4 June: Liechtenstein's II Korps joins I Korps (Clam Gallas) at Magenta, mixing up their brigades.
2. 4 June 1000hrs: MacMahon's II Corps moves off from Turbigo, followed by Camou's Division of the Guard.
3. 1330hrs: Believing MacMahon close at hand, Mellinet's Guard *grenadiers* storm Ponte Nuovo, smashing.
4. 1430hrs Reischach comes up from Abbiategrasso and counterattacks, driving the Guard back onto the river bank, just as:
5. 1530hrs: MacMahon makes ready to launch his own attack.
6. Meanwhile Renault's and Vinoy's divisions hurry through Trecate towards the battlefield, while Austrian reinforcements (III Korps) approach from the south.

deploy whenever resistance appeared likely. Espinasse was still 2.4km short of Marcallo, north-west of Magenta, when the *grenadiers* began their attack along the Naviglio Grande.

MacMahon's other division had been unwittingly responsible for this. The 'Turcos' leading La Motterouge's advance skirmished through Casate and into Boffalora about 1.30pm, their divisional artillery opening fire from the higher ground to the north. These had been the guns heard from the Ticino. MacMahon did not know about the Guard's success at Ponte Nuovo, but from Cuggione church tower his chief of staff could see Kudelka's and Reczniceks's Austrian brigades massing in front of the isolated II Corps. A large gap had opened up between La Motterouge, inclined too far right towards Boffalora, and Espinasse who was stuck at Marcallo. Camou's *voltigeurs* were still an hour behind. MacMahon wanted to gather his forces before engaging what appeared to be superior numbers. He withdrew the 'Turcos' and artillery from Boffalora to a defensive line between Bernate and

At 2.30pm the battle hung in the balance, as vigorous Austrian counterattacks pinned down the Guard at Ponte Nuovo. French reinforcements were still an hour away at Trecate, while MacMahon's turning movement around the Austrian right had yet to make itself felt. Fanti's Sardinians were even further away.

An imaginative interpretation of the advance of Vinoy's 85e Ligne east of the Naviglio Grande, towards Ponte Vecchio. Plenty of Austrian corpses, but no French ones, presumably to get past the Imperial censors. (Author/INW)

Casa Malastalla. Clam Gallas made no move, a curious silence falling across the northern battlefield.

Scenting powder smoke from Ponte Nuovo, MacMahon set off with a platoon of 7e Chasseurs à cheval to hurry up Espinasse. Intent on his mission he burst through hidden groups of Austrian skirmishers so surprised they raised their rifles in surrender. Attacked by *Uhlans*, he charged straight through, without turning a hair. Having ensured the cooperation of Espinasse, MacMahon returned between 3.30 and 4pm to resume the convergent attack on Magenta whose church tower could be seen above the trees. Again La Motterouge advanced on Boffalora, to link up with 2e Grenadiers across their improvised plank bridge. Caught between two fires, the Austrians abandoned Boffalora, falling back on Cascina Nuova.

Clam Gallas tried to exploit MacMahon's overextended front by sending brigades Baltin and Reznicek against Espinasse. The French were advancing either side of the road from Marcallo to Magenta in battalion columns of companies, 2e Zouaves and 71e Ligne on the right, the *Légion étrangère* and 72e Ligne on the left. Guns followed the road, while 11e Chasseurs screened the whole. Clam Gallas's men drove in Espinasse's leading battalions, but failed to reach Marcallo, which the French hastily threw into a state of defence. The wooded terrain favoured the individual initiative of French unit commanders, and the agility of their soldiers, although Colonel de la Chabrière of 2e Régiment étranger was killed going to support the Swiss of 1e Régiment étranger. In a disjointed series of partial combats the French drove off Baltin and Reznicek with volleys and bayonet. The Austrians fell back, rallying along the railway north of Magenta, where they had prepared the station for defence with a ditch and palisades.

While Espinasse drove the Austrians back into Magenta, MacMahon's right-hand division made a quarter turn to its left to attack the walled farm at Cascina Nuova, in cooperation with some of Vinoy's Division, now approaching from Ponte Nuovo. Two of the defending regiments were Hungarian. They behaved badly, losing 1,500 prisoners and a regimental colour, which was found wrapped around the dead body of their colonel. An Austrian lieutenant was bayoneted in the arm trying to make a man face the enemy, and in return shot the fellow with his pistol. Nevertheless, the French advance to the outskirts of Magenta had a nightmarish quality:

The road fought over was covered with debris, feet slipped, and stumbled over the piled up bodies. Bullets struck dead and living alike. All around was heard the cracking of trees broken by bullets and rounds of case shot. At every moment large masses [of enemy] were unexpectedly met, which, when driven off, would obstinately reform, led on by their valiant officers.

Bazancourt vol. I p. 318: author's translation

The final attack on Magenta went in at 7pm, after a pause to regroup. Martimprey of Vinoy's Division was on the right, La Motterouge of II Corps (MacMahon) in the centre with Camou in second line, and Espinasse in two columns on the left. One of these advanced directly along the road from Marcallo, the other approached indirectly from the east, by the Milan road. MacMahon had commanded the *Légion étrangère* back in the 1840s. Now, as the troops awaited the order to advance, he added another legend to their history with the *bon mot*: 'Voici la Légion. L'affaire est dans le sac!' – 'The Legion is here. The game is in the bag.'

Meanwhile Général Auger, MacMahon's artillery chief, had massed the corps reserve batteries with La Motterouge's two divisional batteries, perhaps 39 guns, along the railway embankment, the first position allowing such a deployment. These crossed their fire with another 30 guns beyond the Naviglio, the shells ploughing up Magenta's barricaded streets, and ricocheting off loopholed garden walls. The effect was decisive. Magenta became a scene of chaos, as shattered detachments of every arm of the Austrian Army fell back from the town's outskirts to jam streets with broken weapons, bodies and abandoned equipment.

Leading his men against a strongpoint, Espinasse dismounted when his horse stumbled over some corpses. His ADC was shot immediately, his body found later leaning against a wall with ten bullet wounds. Espinasse himself was killed, like the old *zouave* he was, beating with his sword pommel on the door of a house full of Austrian *Jäger*, whose accurate rifle fire caused many casualties. Streetfighting continued until 8pm, well after most of the defenders had withdrawn to Corbetta or Robecco. The retreat was covered by Lilia's unengaged division of VII Korps (Zobel) and Brigade Dormus of V Korps (Stadion), which had just arrived after a heroic march. Down by the canal, Schwarzenberg's last counterattack at Ponte Vecchio faded away, discouraged by the approaching trumpet calls of Trochu's Division of III Corps (Canrobert).

French troops advance on Magenta from the north, *zouaves* on the left, infantry in the old *bonnets de police* on the right. A generalized image, but giving an impression of the now-built-up countryside north of Magenta. (Author/lemonde)

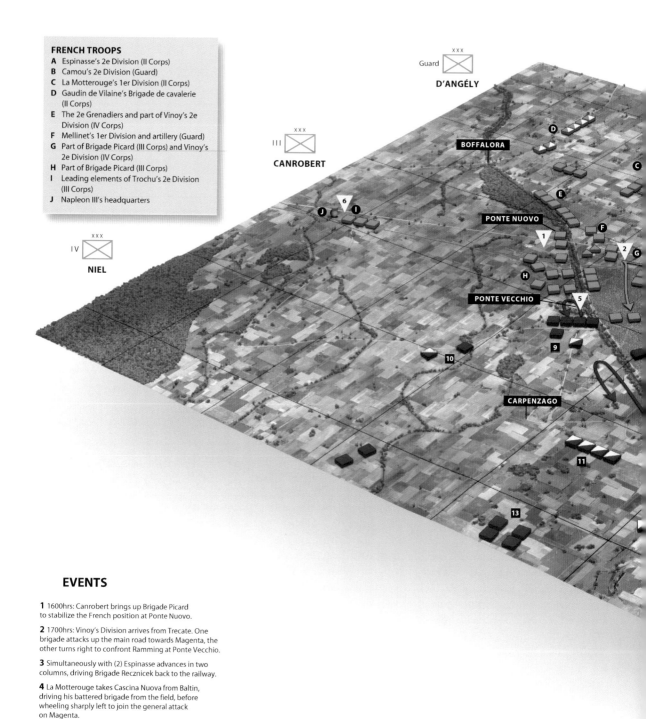

FRENCH TROOPS

- **A** Espinasse's 2e Division (II Corps)
- **B** Camou's 2e Division (Guard)
- **C** La Motterouge's 1er Division (II Corps)
- **D** Gaudin de Vilaine's Brigade de cavalerie (II Corps)
- **E** The 2e Grenadiers and part of Vinoy's 2e Division (IV Corps)
- **F** Mellinet's 1er Division and artillery (Guard)
- **G** Part of Brigade Picard (III Corps) and Vinoy's 2e Division (IV Corps)
- **H** Part of Brigade Picard (III Corps)
- **I** Leading elements of Trochu's 2e Division (III Corps)
- **J** Napleon III's headquarters

Guard
D'ANGÉLY

III CANROBERT

IV NIEL

BOFFALORA

PONTE NUOVO

PONTE VECCHIO

CARPENZAGO

EVENTS

1 1600hrs: Canrobert brings up Brigade Picard to stabilize the French position at Ponte Nuovo.

2 1700hrs: Vinoy's Division arrives from Trecate. One brigade attacks up the main road towards Magenta, the other turns right to confront Ramming at Ponte Vecchio.

3 Simultaneously with (2) Espinasse advances in two columns, driving Brigade Recznicek back to the railway.

4 La Motterouge takes Cascina Nuova from Baltin, driving his battered brigade from the field, before wheeling sharply left to join the general attack on Magenta.

5 West of the canal, Picard fought Hartung and Dürfeld to a standstill by 1900hrs.

6 2000hrs: Trochu arrives to consolidate the position after dark. Napoleon goes to bed unaware of his victory.

MAGENTA, 4 JUNE 1859: THE FRENCH PINCERS CLOSE IN

The desperate stand of the French Guard at Ponte Nuovo soaked up Austrian reserves and gained time for French reinforcements to arrive. In the last hours of daylight, MacMahon's Algerians smashed Gyulai's northern flank, and stormed into Magenta.

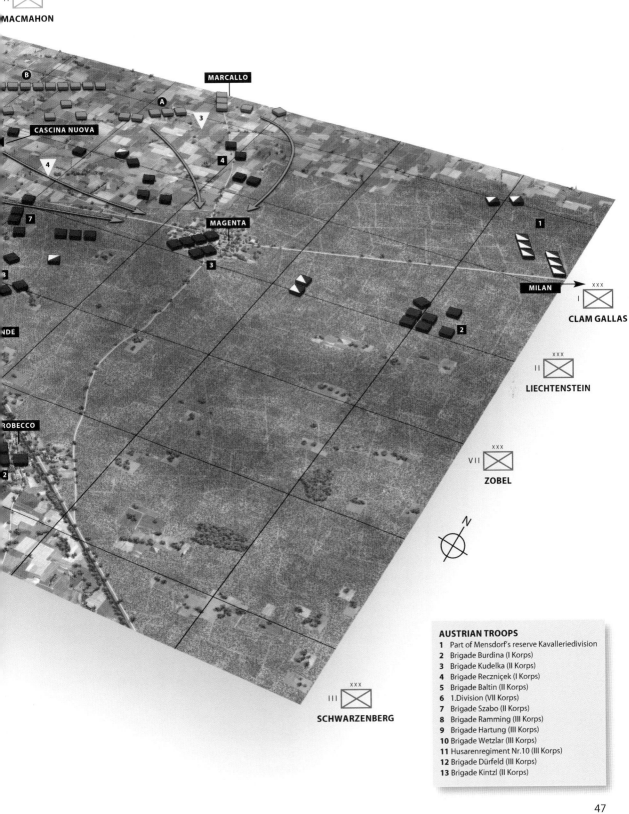

Note: Gridlines are shown at intervals of 1km/1093yds

MACMAHON

MARCALLO

B

A

CASCINA NUOVA

MAGENTA

MILAN

CLAM GALLAS

LIECHTENSTEIN

ZOBEL

N

SCHWARZENBERG

AUSTRIAN TROOPS
1 Part of Mensdorf's reserve Kavalleriedivision
2 Brigade Burdina (I Korps)
3 Brigade Kudelka (II Korps)
4 Brigade Reczniçek (I Korps)
5 Brigade Baltin (II Korps)
6 1.Division (VII Korps)
7 Brigade Szabo (II Korps)
8 Brigade Ramming (III Korps)
9 Brigade Hartung (III Korps)
10 Brigade Wetzlar (III Korps)
11 Husarenregiment Nr.10 (III Korps)
12 Brigade Dürfeld (III Korps)
13 Brigade Kintzl (II Korps)

Cascina Nuova seen from the Boffalora–Magenta road. Brigade Baltin defended the buildings against La Motterouge's Division, before retreating towards the viewer across the field, where many surrendered. (Author/photo)

As usual the Austrians had wasted their strength in flanking detachments that achieved little. Urban's flying column turned back from chasing Garibaldi, but failed to intervene against MacMahon's open flank. On the Austrians' extreme left Brigade Wetzlar of III Korps (Schwarzenberg) wandered about the rice fields, but never posed a serious threat to the slender French lifeline across the Ticino. MacMahon's delay, dangerous as it appeared, ensured the most decisive result for his attack. Espinasse's wide turning movement drove Magenta's defenders back into the angle between the main road and canal, where their densely packed reserves provided a fine target for the crossfire between Auger's guns and the Guard artillery.

As firing died down, Colonel Toulongeon, one of Napoleon's orderly officers, caught up with MacMahon, finding him quite unaware of the close-run action along the canal. Napoleon III was equally oblivious of the fate of II Corps. He went to bed fully clothed in a dilapidated inn at San Martino, surrounded by broken-down transport and ambulances full of wounded soldiers. Only when Colonel Toulongeon awoke him much later did the emperor learn how MacMahon's victorious advance had saved the Allies from another divided battle.

THE EVACUATION OF LOMBARDY

So close was the battle of Magenta that at 8.30pm Gyulai issued orders to resume the fight the next day. The French had gained little permanent advantage from the action, while neither side's losses were sufficiently heavy to be decisive. Remote from events at Abbiategrasso, Gyulai did not realize the extent of his army's disorganization, as revealed by the huge number of Austrian missing:

	Killed	Wounded	Missing	Total
French	707	3,223	655	4,585
Austrian	1,368	4,358	4,500	10,226

Reports received during the night destroyed Gyulai's illusions. Clam Gallas and Zobel (I and VII Korps) had already retreated on Milan, away from the rest of the army. Gyulai recognized the inevitable, and issued orders

French *chasseurs* or legionnaires (both wore the short *capote-tunique*) attacking Magenta church. Any solid building was likely to become a strongpoint; note the troops firing from the tower and roof. (RNM/ILN)

for withdrawal, leaving behind a battlefield littered with 12,000 rifles and 30,000 knapsacks, evidence of Austrian demoralization.

The Allies spent 5 June reorganizing, and collecting both sides' wounded. Napoleon recognized his victory in the Imperial fashion, promoting Regnaud St Jean d'Angély and MacMahon *maréchaux de France*, the latter with the title Duc de Magenta. The Allies did not reach Milan until 8 June, to be greeted by rapturous crowds. Meanwhile the Austrian Army retreated eastwards, in three great columns. On the right (under Benedek), I, VII and VIII Korps (Clam Gallas, Zobel, Benedek) and Mensdorff's cavalry moved back to Montechiaro by Lodi, Soncino and Manerbio. In the centre (under Schwarzenberg), II and III Korps (Liechtenstein and Schwarzenberg) with the garrison of Pavia went to Valeggio, Volta and Roverbello, moving by Borghetta, Bertonico and Robecco d'Oglio. On the left, V and IX Korps (Stadion, Schaafsgottsche) went with the heavy baggage to Mantua, moving via Pizzighettone, Cremona and Piadena.

Gyulai hoped to hold the river Chiese between Lonato and Castiglione, within easy reach of the Quadrilateral and the reinforcements concentrating there. He abandoned the Austrian fortresses along the Po, spiking their guns and choking the river with rice tipped out from their magazines. Benedek's VIII Korps acted as rearguard, throwing out Brigade Roden to Melegnano on the main road between Lodi and Milan to cover the exposed flank.

STREET-FIGHTING IN MAGENTA, 4 JUNE 1859 (pp. 50–51)

French troops of MacMahon's II Corps fight their way down Magenta's narrow streets on the evening of the battle, under close-range rifle fire. *Zouaves* and *chasseurs à pied* stand ready to storm a house, while engineers break the door open with axes (1), and further waves of troops press on down the street. Just right of centre, a *chasseur* officer (2) has been shot by an invisible marksman. The only Austrians to be seen are casualties (3), caught in the open by the first rush. Every house forms a miniature fortress, with thick battered stone walls beneath the stucco, shuttered windows, and massive double gates leading into an inner courtyard (4).

Three types of French soldier can be seen:
Chasseurs à pied (5) in dark blue with yellow distinctions and green épaulettes. Formed in the 1840s as specialist light infantry they carry a short muzzle-loading percussion rifle, the Model 1859 carabine d'Orléans, with the wavy M/1842 sabre-baïonette, fixed on the right of the muzzle so the flat of the blade is parallel to the ground when held at the present. Light blue neck scarves were a popular campaign accessory, as was the officer's sash, the waistcoat worn open to show the shirt and black silk bow tie. All unnecessary equipment has been dumped at the start

of the action, making French troops slow to follow up a success, until they have recovered their packs.

Zouaves (6) in their characteristic 'Turkish' style copied from the Arabs of Algeria, where the corps was first raised in the 1830s: red *chechia* or fez, with dark blue tassel, worn pushed well back on the head; dark blue woollen *veste* or short jacket edged in red; baggy summer weight trousers in off-white linen. Like *chasseurs*, *zouaves* wore leather *jambières* round the lower leg above white buttoned gaiters, sometimes giving the misleading appearance of bare legs. They carry a full-length rifled percussion musket with triangular socket bayonet. *Zouave* officers (7) followed metropolitan line infantry styles, with red kepis and baggy trousers.

Sapeurs du génie (8): every French division included a company of engineers, whose duties included breaking into enemy occupied buildings. Dressed in dark blue with red distinctions, they have the line infantry-style *capote* or overcoat, cut loose and comfortable, skirts buttoned back clear of the legs. Like the *chasseurs* they wear neck scarves and dark blue woollen kepis, with a square leather visor but no chinstrap.

The combat of Melegnano, 8 July

Meanwhile the Allies had lost touch with the enemy, so Napoleon ordered a reconnaissance towards Lodi. Baraguey d'Hilliers was to take his own I Corps and MacMahon's II Corps down to Melegnano on 8 June to check whether the Austrians were really abandoning Lombardy, or preparing a counterstroke.

Baraguey and MacMahon agreed that the latter should move down the main road first, as far as San Giulano, just north of Melegnano, and then across the river Lambro to turn Roden's right flank. I Corps would follow to menace Melegnano from the north and west. Unfortunately Baraguey suffered the usual delays: II Corps' transport blocked the main road, and the neighbouring rice fields were impassable. Bazaine's Division of I Corps did not reach Melegnano until 3.30pm, his column providing a dense target for Austrian guns firing straight down the road. This, with the lateness of the hour, persuaded the temperamentally impatient Baraguey to attack at once, without waiting for MacMahon's turning movement.

Melegnano straggles either side of the Lambro, with an old castle in the western half, partly surrounded by a moat. Brigade Roden had spent considerable energy on its defences, building a firing platform inside the two-metre walls of the churchyard, and entangling the main road from Milan with cut-down trees. Besides his own troops, Roden could count on Brigade Boer behind the town. For once the Austrians fought well. They threw back the 1er Zouaves, who led Bazaine's attack, and launched ferocious counterattacks. De Ladmirault's Division came up behind Bazaine, and tried a closer flanking movement, but the farm roads petered out, the ground turned to slush, and the Lambro proved unfordable. Ladmirault's men had to improvise bridges from carts and tree trunks, before forcing the Austrians back upon the castle, where their marksmen took cover amongst the orchards lining its walls. Baraguey and Bazaine directed savage street fighting in which 33e Ligne almost lost their eagle. Not until MacMahon's shells burst on the road to Lodi did the Austrians give up. Brigade Boer covered Roden's retreat, occupying the castle until all Austrian troops east of the Lambro had been evacuated.

Presentation of captured Austrian standards to the newly promoted Maréchal MacMahon after Magenta. French soldiers clear the dead for burial beside the railway, then on the outskirts of town. (Author/INW)

Excluding prisoners the Austrians inflicted more casualties than they suffered, a disproportion attributable to Baraguey's haste. On the other hand the Austrians should not have awaited such a heavy attack, as they were retreating anyway. Losses were as follows:

	Killed	Wounded	Missing	Total
French	153	734	64	951
Austrian	120	240	1,114	1,474

Two-thirds of the French casualties came from 1er Zouaves who lost a third of their number. Napoleon had no stomach for such carnage. In future the Allies would advance in a solid mass, under the emperor's direct control. Ironically this lack of manoeuvre would lead to a head-on encounter bloodier than Magenta, but not a lot more decisive.

Retreat and reorganization

Gyulai's retreat was largely undisturbed, except for skirmishes between Garibaldi and Urban, who narrowly avoided being caught between the insurgents and the Sardinians at Milan. By 16 June Gyulai was back on the Chiese, supported by fresh forces under Franz Josef at Verona. The Austrian emperor had arrived in Italy on 30 May to organize the rear, while Gyulai directed operations at the front. On 18 June, however, Gyulai resigned in favour of Graf Schlick, a Napoleonic veteran. The Kaiser took personal command of all Austrian forces in Italy. These now formed two armies, as follows:

Erste Armee (Wimpffen) consisting of:	Zweite Armee (Schlick) consisting of:
II Korps (Liechtenstein)	I Korps (Clam Gallas)
III Korps (Schwarzenberg)	V Korps (Stadion)
IX Korps (Schaafsgottsche)	VII Korps (Zobel)
XI Korps (Weigl)	VIII Korps (Benedek)
Kavalleriedivision (Zedtwitz)	Kavalleriedivision (Mensdorff)

An additional X Korps (Wernhardt) was detached to secure the lower reaches of the Po. It took no part in the battle.

Hess was in nominal charge of operations, but he was saddled with a deputy chief of staff, GM Ramming, whom he detested. Grünne continued to exert his malign influence, disputing Hess's right to command, and consigning him to a broken-down carriage at the tail end of the Imperial cortège. Zweite Armee eventually retired over the Mincio on 20/21 June, and lined up between Lake Garda and Mantua, apparently intending to dispute the river crossings.

The Allies advanced cautiously, closed up ready to fight. Marches were short but exhausting, made painful by congestion, dust and intense heat. There were four major rivers to cross, swollen by the recent rain, which hindered replacement of demolished bridges. While the Austrians debated whether to hold the Chiese, the Allies closed up south of Brescia. The Sardinians were on the left, the French on their right: I Corps (Baraguey), II Corps (MacMahon), and IV (Niel) in the first line, followed by the Guard and III Corps (Canrobert). On the 21st it became clear the Austrians had retreated across the Mincio, and the Allies moved up to the Chiese.

On the right, IV Corps (Niel) was at Carpenodolo, east of the river, the cavalry divisions of Partouneaux and Desvaux covering the flanks; III Corps (Canrobert) stood just behind on the west bank. In the centre, II Corps (MacMahon) stopped at Montechiaro; I Corps (Baraguey) was immediately behind, but still on the west bank. On the left, the Sardinian 3ª Division (Mollard) stood at Desenzano by Lake Garda; 1ª and 5ª divisions (Durando and Cucchiari) were at Lonato. Held in reserve were the Guard and Imperial headquarters at Castenedolo, as well as Vittorio Emmanuele at Calcinato with his 2ª Division (Fanti); Cialdini's 4ª Division was detached to support Garibaldi in the mountains.

MacMahon occupied Castiglione on 22 June, the Guard infantry replacing him at Montechiaro. Its cavalry stayed at Castenedolo, ten kilometres behind the rest of the army. That day and the next were spent examining the country between the Chiese and Mincio, including a hot air balloon ascent from Castiglione. French divisional commanders received fresh maps of the countryside ahead. Considerable Austrian activity was observed, but after so many retreats this was interpreted as patrols. No one could imagine that having given up their strong position on the Chiese without a fight, the Austrians would offer battle with the Mincio at their backs, a far poorer position than the one they had just left. That, however, was exactly what they intended to do.

THE BATTLE OF SOLFERINO

The district around Solferino well suited a battle between 250,000 men commanded by two emperors and a king. The ground allowed large masses of troops to move freely, its undulations providing cover for skirmishers and ample fields of fire for artillery. In the southern half of the battlefield, the Medole plain favoured cavalry and horse artillery, while manoeuvres could be directed from the high ground to the north.

Eighteen kilometres from south to north, the battlefield lies between the rivers Mincio and Chiese to the east and west respectively, and Lake Garda on the north. A steep ridge cuts diagonally across the quadrilateral formed by the two streams. Along it lies a series of villages. Starting from Castiglione in the west, there was Grole halfway in a fold of ground, then Solferino, in a cleft just east of the highest point of the ridge, then San Cassiano spreading up the slope beyond. Further on, Cavriana's scattered houses nestled in the heart of the hillside. Finally came Volta on the last hilltop before the Mincio, with a superb view of the plain to the west.

North of the ridge, small round moranic hills run down towards Lake Garda, their slopes covered with the usual mixture of vines, mulberry trees and corn. The Sole and Redone streams divide the high ground, separating Solferino in the south from Madonna della Scoperta in the centre and San Martino in the north. Communications reflect the diagonal slant of the ground, major routes running north-west to south-east, connected by smaller side roads. The Milan–Verona railway and main road follow the southern shore of Lake Garda to Peschiera, now supplemented by a motorway. Another main road runs slantwise from Castiglione through Guidizzolo, crossing the Mincio at Goito. Minor roads run along the ridge from Castiglione to converge on Solferino.

Solferino is in the very centre of the battlefield, equidistant from the Chiese and Mincio, halfway between Lake Garda in the north and Castel Goffredo in the south. A large tower known as the Spia d'Italia, or Spy of Italy, occupies a height west of Solferino, giving a view of the whole battlefield. Solferino's

Napoleon III crosses the river Chiese on an improvised trestle bridge. The Allies had to cross numerous rivers during their advance across Lombardy, their engineers replacing demolished bridges as they went. (Author/INW)

The tower, convent and cemetery at Solferino: a party of English officers study the ground in October 1859. The outlying village of Pozzo Catena lies in the hollow, the Monte di Cipressi further to the right. (Author/Miller)

main street is particularly difficult to enter from Castiglione, as the approach runs along a knife-edged ridge past a high-walled cemetery, before turning sharp left and right between an orchard at the back of the cemetery and the convent church of San Nicola, itself part of the Piazza Castello or Castle Square. Enclosed by massive walls six to nine metres high with arched gateways either end, this formed a deep position of great natural strength. It was flanked on the defenders' right rear by the church of San Pietro and on the left by a long narrow hill, the Monte de Cipressi, running down from the Spia d'Italia. These features, joined up with hedges and barricades, blocked all routes into Solferino from the west. Together they formed an immense outwork covering the terraced slopes of Cavriana, where the Austrians massed their reserves.

Further south a great plain, the Campo di Medole, extends beyond the battlefield as far as the river Oglio, which joins the Po south of Mantua. The plain was waterless and relatively devoid of trees, compared with other parts of Northern Italy. Cultivated with maize, wheat, barley or rye, it presented few obstacles to troop movements beyond a few insignificant depressions made by streams that periodically drained the hills to the north. A greater problem was the difficulty of maintaining direction through the tall standing crops, with no particular landmark to head for. This flat ground suited both the rifled guns of the French and the massed manoeuvres of the Austrians, to whom the plain was as familiar as Hyde Park was to the British Foot Guards. What cover there was consisted of gardens and thickets around the villages, whose red roofs stood out against the greenery. In the absence of other features, settlements such as Guidizzolo, Rebecco and Báite (sometimes spelled Baete) became the scene of desperate fighting. An irrigation canal, the Seriola Marchionale, runs diagonally from near Castiglione through Medole to Ceresara. A much less significant obstacle than the Naviglio Grande at Magenta, the Seriola Marchionale formed the southern edge of the battlefield. Little fighting occurred beyond it.

Advance to contact

The Austrian retreat across the Mincio was a short-lived victory for the realists among Franz Josef's professional advisers who wanted to remain on the defensive within the Quadrilateral and wear the Allies down. On 22 June

the Kaiser ordered a combined advance over the Mincio, across which Gyulai's dispirited troops had so recently withdrawn. The aim was to catch the Allies crossing the Chiese and win a tactical success before further Allied reinforcements arrived. The French V Corps (Prince Napoleon) was moving up from Tuscany, while the Sardinian 4ª Division (Cialdini), might return from supporting Garibaldi.

The advance of the Austrian right (Zweite Armee under Schlick) through the high ground between the Volta and Lake Garda was to pin the enemy frontally, while Erste Armee and the reserve cavalry divisions wheeled up across the Campo di Medole. The whole army would then launch a concentric attack on Montechiaro, where the Allied forces were supposed to be. Hess asserted that such an enveloping movement would take too long, the Allies having ample time to catch the Austrians on the march, and smash their over-extended centre. Grünne and Ramming, however, supported the scheme, and on 23 June the Austrian armies marched back across the Mincio bridges, Zweite Armee at 9am, Erste Armee an hour later. Officers and men were impatient for action to avenge their previous defeats. The order of march was as follows, from the right:

Formation	Route	Bridge
Zweite Armee (Schlick):	Headquarters to Volta	
VIII (Benedek)	Peschiera–Pozzolengo	Salionze
V (Stadion)	Salionze–Solferino	Valeggio
I (Clam Gallas) (following V Korps)	Villafranca–Cavriana	Valeggio
Cavalry (Mensdorff) (following III Korps)	Villafranca–Cavriana	Ferri
VII (Zobel) (following Mensdorff)	Villafranca–Volta	Ferri
Erste Armee (Wimpffen):	Headquarters to Cereta, near Volta	
III (Schwarzenberg)	Pozzolo–Guidizzolo	Ferri
IX (Schaafsgottsche)	Goito–Rebecco/Medole	Goito
Cavalry (Zedtwitz) (Brigade Lauingen only)	Villafranca–Medole	Goito
XI (Weigl) (following Zedtwitz)	Roverbella–Castel Grimaldo	Goito

The battle of Solferino, approach to contact, 23–24 June

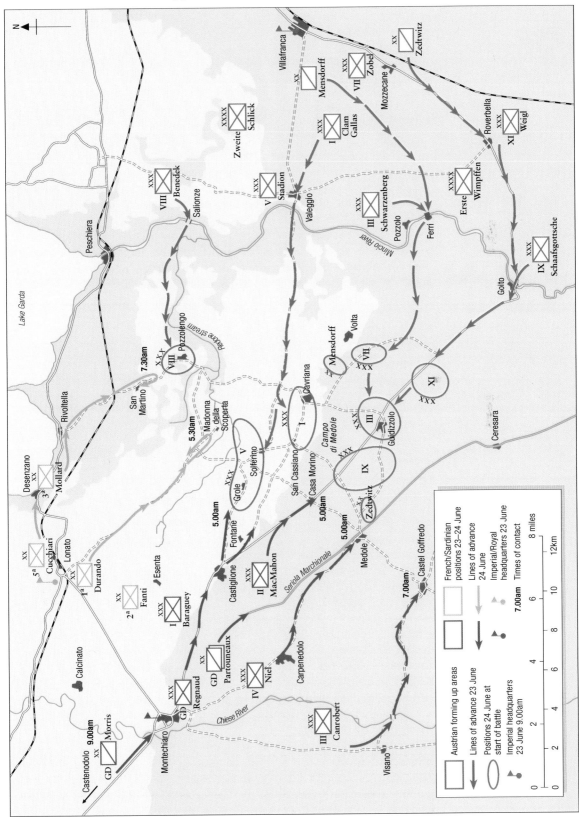

A contemporary panorama of the battlefield from the west, i.e. the Allied point of view, showing Lake Garda (far left), the high ground along which the leftmost French corps advanced (centre), and the Medole plain away to the right. (Author/INW)

Liechtenstein's II Korps remained at Mantua, sending Jellaçic's Division to Marcaria on the Oglio River to threaten the French right. Both Austrian armies reached their objectives during the afternoon of 23 June. No one at Imperial headquarters expected a fight on the 24th, although hardly six kilometres separated the hostile armies, and no orders were issued against that contingency. Baggage remained with the troops, hindering their already naturally sluggish movements. Unfortunately for the Austrians, the Allies did exactly as Hess predicted. On 23 June Napoleon III ordered a fresh advance next morning. Dispositions were as follows, from north to south:

Formation	Route
Sardinian Army:	Lonato/Desenzano–Pozzolengo, except:
1ª (Durando)	Lonato–Madonna della Scoperta
2ª (Fanti)	Between Esenta and Lonato in reserve
French Army:	
I (Baraguey)	Esenta–Solferino, along the ridge
II (MacMahon)	Castiglione–Cavriana, by the main road
IV (Niel)	Carpenedolo–Guidizzolo via Medole
III (Canrobert)	Mezzane–Medole via Castel Goffredo
Guard (Regnaud)	Montechiaro–Castiglione, in reserve
Guard cavalry (Morriss)	Carpenedolo–Guidizzolo directly

As the Austrians held most of the Allied objectives, a collision was inevitable. Both sides would be equally surprised. The Allies, however, wrong-footed their enemy by moving off very early, between 2 and 3am, to avoid the heat of the day. The French marched tactically. Transport was left to come on later, so the fighting troops at Solferino would not be delayed by traffic jams as they had been at Magenta. Catching the Austrians still cooking breakfast, the French gained the initiative, and kept it. The Sardinians had the harder task of taking the more distant and highly defensible ground towards Peschiera, and enjoyed less success.

Summary of the battle

Solferino was not the result of any grand strategic combination. The two armies had blundered up against one another, along roughly parallel fronts. Accidental encounters flared up along the whole front, preventing either side gaining a decision by manoeuvre. The battle would be won by whichever side first seized control of events.

Not surprisingly the French proved quicker on their feet, instinctively concentrating on their centre, a process Napoleon III hastened rather than initiated. The Austrians persisted with their original plan, but failed to concentrate, allowing three French corps to smash their centre in a concerted attack. Although the Austrians had as many troops between Solferino and Cavriana as the French, Schlick's corps engaged successively, and were defeated in detail. Meanwhile Niel's IV Corps in the south fought twice its own number of Austrians to gain time for the breakthrough in the centre. Again the Austrians failed to impose unity of action on their superior numbers, bringing up brigades of different corps piecemeal. The inadequate support Niel felt he had received from III Corps (Canrobert) during the day resulted in heated exchanges between the two commanders after the battle. To the north, Benedek's reinforced VIII Korps fought a separate action against a series of disjointed Sardinian attacks around San Martino and Madonna della Scoperta. As usual several Austrian formations did nothing, the reserve artillery apparently playing no part in the battle.

Solferino lacked the dramatic ups and downs of Magenta, almost all the troops being present from the start. Total numbers engaged were:

Army	Infantry	Cavalry	Guns
Austrians	119,783	9,490	429
French	82,935	9,162	240
Sardinians	37,174	1,562	80

The table excludes: Austrian II Korps (Liechtenstein), French V Corps (Prince Napoleon), part of French III Corps (Canrobert), the Sardinian cavalry reserve and 4ª Division (Cialdini), which saw no action. Forces were distributed unevenly, as follows:

1) Benedek had six brigades in the north, with part of V Korps (Stadion), to defend a frontage of some 7.2km against eight Sardinian brigades (28,558 Austrians with 88 guns vs. 38,736 Sardinians with 80 guns).

2) Between Solferino and Cavriana, three Austrian corps received the attack of three French corps on a frontage of only 2.3km giving the astonishing troop density on the attacking side of 22 men per metre (46,716 Austrians with 164 guns vs. 55,311 French with 144 guns).

The Piazza Castello seen from above: the cemetery's eastern wall is extreme left, beyond the orchard with its rows of fruit trees. The whole complex formed a great defensive outwork protecting the Austrian centre. (Author/photo)

3) Before Medole, three Austrian corps opposed one French corps, reinforced by a second, on a frontage of 3.6km (53,999 Austrians with 177 guns vs. 21,026 French (rising to 36,786) with 96 guns).

Napoleon III was in Montechiaro when the first shots were heard. As he dashed to the front in his postchaise, he received reports showing that a great battle was imminent. Having arrived at Castiglione, Napoleon took immediate control of the situation, climbing a church tower to view the battlefield before visiting his central corps commanders to coordinate their movements. From the tower he could see the whole country, from Lake Garda, blue in the morning sunshine, to the hazy Mincio valley and the steeples of Mantua. The Austrians' wide front and reports of Liechtenstein's turning movement in the south suggested the enemy line would be thin, inviting a classic Napoleonic rupture of their centre.

Napoleon III's first step was to close up his right and left on the centre, while developing an attack on the high ground around Solferino. On such a far-flung battlefield, however, it took time to put his orders into effect. The cavalry and artillery of the Guard only left Castenodolo at 9am. They would not be available for hours. Baraguey's I Corps attacked Solferino all morning without support. Beyond his left, the Sardinian 3[a] and 5[a] divisions were beaten in detail, drawing away Fanti's 2[a] Division to help them. MacMahon could not assist Baraguey until 11am, when Niel's IV Corps freed II Corps to wheel left to capture San Cassiano. This cut off the Austrian defenders of Solferino, which Baraguey took about 2pm with the help of the Guard. The French then rolled up the line of hills between Solferino and Cavriana, which fell at 5pm. At that point a violent storm ended the main battle, leaving the Allies holding a line roughly parallel to the initial encounters, but up to six kilometres in advance of it.

The Austrian reaction was less coherent. When his outposts came under fire at 5am, the IX Korps commander (Schaafsgottsche) was unwilling to move off until his men had eaten their first meal for 24 hours. The Austrians at Medole held out for three hours against Luzy's division of IV Corps (Niel), their brigade commander, Blumencron, ignoring their calls for help. The entire army lacked a head until 11am. Franz Josef simply disappeared. With an instinct *The Times* described as more canine than human, the Imperial staff hunted back and forth until, six hours into the battle, they ran their master to earth on the Monte Roccolo, calmly discussing the chances of the day with FML Hess.

Even then the Austrians displayed little generalship. Individual brigades came up, but were never employed in any connected manner. When the Austrian centre fell back after the loss of Solferino, the three corps on their left attempted to combine against Niel, but only succeeded in stopping Niel's own attacks upon Guidizzolo. Benedek alone held his ground, but his isolated success was insufficient to reverse the general result.

The detailed narrative of the battle forms three distinct sections:

1) Benedek's stand against the Sardinians between Lake Garda and Solferino.

2) The French advance in the centre upon Solferino and Cavriana, conducted by I and II corps, and the Guard.

3) Defensive operations south of the main Goito road, conducted primarily by French IV Corps (Niel), supported by III Corps (Canrobert).

The Sardinian assault on San Martino, 24 June (about 7pm)

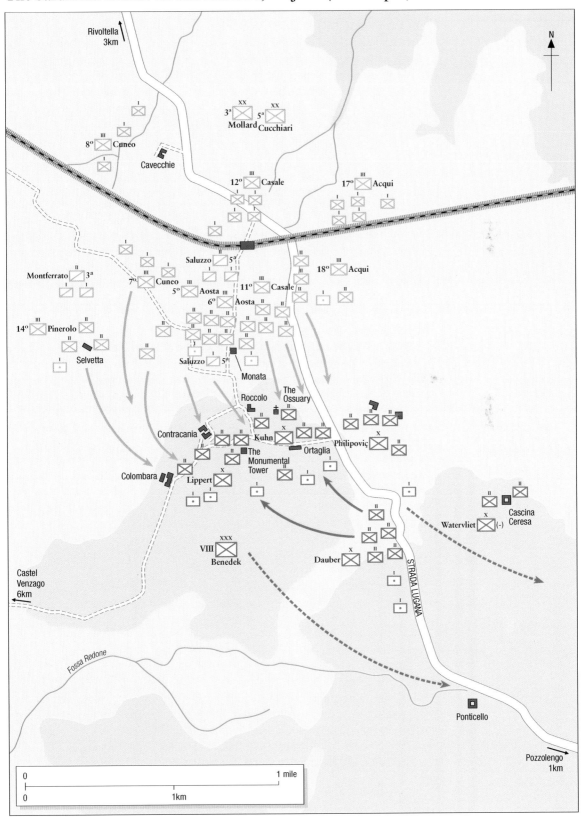

SAN MARTINO DELLA BATTAGLIA

The Sardinians advanced in three columns screened by strong reconnoitring parties, which were drawn into premature and ill-coordinated attacks. The hilly terrain prevented mutual support, while Vittorio Emmanuele spent his day watching the French attack on Solferino, abdicating control of his own army. The leading Sardinian divisions advanced as follows, from left to right:

Division	Line of march
5ª (Cucchiari)	via Rivoltella to Pozzolengo
3ª (Mollard)	south of the railway to San Martino
1ª (Durando)	via Castel Venzago to Madonna della Scoperta

Durando reached the hamlet of Madonna della Scoperta about 5.30am, but found it occupied by Stadion's V Korps. The defenders pushed Durando's advanced guard back down the Lonato road, beyond the crossroads shown on modern maps at point 117. The Sardinian main body left Lonato at 7am, but took five hours to march the ten kilometres to Madonna della Scoperta. Durando's *granatieri* were left all morning to sustain the action unsupported. By the time his reserves arrived, the Austrians had withdrawn, following the French success at Solferino.

Meanwhile, Cucchiari's advanced guard had met the enemy at Ponticello, one-and-a-half kilometres short of Pozzolengo, at 7.30am. Benedek used four of his six brigades to drive the Sardinians back four kilometres beyond the high ground, which he then occupied himself. Shaped like a flattened lozenge the hill known as San Martino was a formidable position. Rising 32m from where the railway crosses the Strada Lugana, the Pozzolengo–Rivoltella road, it was large enough to accommodate numerous troops. Steep slopes to the north formed a natural rampart strengthened by stone buildings and clumps of pine trees. The Sardinians in the sector outnumbered Benedek's four brigades by 25,000 men to 20,000, but throughout the day failed to exploit their numerical superiority. One Piedmontese brigade after another launched unsuccessful piecemeal assaults against the bloodstained slopes of San Martino.

The final Sardinian attack at San Martino, depicted by a contemporary artist, showing the steep terrain dotted with trees and farm buildings: Monata (centre), la Roccolo (behind), and Contracania (halfway up the slope to the right) are all recognizable. (Author/Bossoli)

The first to try was Brigata Cuneo of Mollard's 3ᵃ Division, which took the lower spurs of San Martino hill at 9am. Austrian bayonet attacks soon drove them back to the railway. The artillery of Cucchiari's 5ᵃ Division trotted up from Rivoltella ahead of its infantry, to stabilize the situation, assisted by a gallant charge of the Saluzzo light horse regiment. Both Cucchiari's brigades renewed the action about 10am. They captured Roccolo Farm at noon, but lacked the reserves to exploit their success. When Brigata Pinerolo of 3ᵃ Division arrived at 1pm, it was just in time to see Cucchiari's leading battalions give way under the fire of 30 pieces of artillery, unmasked against them at a range of 230m from the top of the hill. At such short ranges the Austrian SB guns could fire case to devastating effect. The whole of the 5ᵃ Division retreated from the field, only stopping at Rivoltella. Mollard deployed his two brigades along the railway, and awaited reinforcements. Benedek did not press his advantage, being doubtful of the situation on his left at Solferino, so for several hours there was a lull. While the Sardinians had exhausted themselves in piecemeal frontal attacks, Benedek used his reserves effectively, always menacing the enemy's flanks. At a personal level Benedek demonstrated his rare ability to motivate the Austrian soldier, calling out to the survivors of a successful bayonet attack that he could kiss the lot of them.

Fanti's 2ᵃ Division had remained in reserve near Esenta when the other three advanced. Ten kilometres behind both wings of the Sardinian Army, it was too far away to lend timely assistance to either. At 11am Fanti received orders to support 1ᵃ Division (Durando), whose repulse at Madonna della Scoperta had exposed the left flank of the French Army, still locked in a desperate struggle at Solferino. Grim news from San Martino, however, persuaded Vittorio Emmanuele to split his reserve. La Marmora took Brigata Piemonte to Madonna della Scoperta, while Brigata Aosta went to San Martino. Receiving this reinforcement about 4pm, Mollard re-opened the battle. He placed his own Brigata Pinerolo on the right and the newly arrived Brigata Aosta on the left. Each brigade put one four-battalion regiment in the firing line, with another in support. In contrast with previous ill-coordinated attacks, Mollard ordered a convergent assault, following a pre-arranged signal. The re-formed Brigata Cuneo acted as reserve.

The Austrian collapse at Solferino forced Benedek to detach Brigade Reichlin to Pozzolengo to cover his left rear. As soon as Stadion's V Korps had evacuated Madonna della Scoperta, La Marmora occupied the hamlet, pushing on eastwards past Monte Torricello towards Pozzolengo with Fanti's Brigata Piemonte. Menaced on three sides, Benedek was in a most dangerous position. Following a short interruption at 5pm caused by the storm, Mollard's Brigata Pinerolo skirmished forwards, clearing the farmhouses between the railway and the high ground. Before San Martino, the Italians were checked again by point-blank artillery fire. Heavy losses included both of the Brigata Pinerolo's regimental commanders. Nevertheless, the surviving attackers clung onto Monata Farm halfway up the slope, while Cucchiari's battered 5ᵃ Division came up into a precarious position on the extreme left of the Allied army, turning Benedek's far right. At sunset five Sardinian brigades, in their first combined attack of the day, forced their way onto San Martino from all sides. Benedek had orders to retire, and grudgingly gave way. All firing ceased about 9pm, Benedek making good his retreat to Salionze. The last Austrian troops recrossed the Mincio at 3am on the 25th.

Both sides claimed a victory at San Martino. The Sardinians suffered 20 per cent casualties, a higher loss rate than any French division: 691 killed,

3,572 wounded and 1,258 missing. They certainly took the Pozzolengo Plateau, but in a manner that reflected better upon the tenacity of the troops than the skill of their leaders. Benedek's defence, which cost VIII Korps 2,615 casualties, was the only bright spot in an otherwise disastrous day for Austrian arms.

DECISION IN THE CENTRE

Baraguey and MacMahon moved off from Esenta and Castiglione about 3am on 24 June, heading for Solferino and Cavriana respectively. There was no good road along the ridge, so only Ladmirault's Division of I Corps marched that way, taking four guns. Forey's and Bazaine's divisions went via Castiglione with the rest of the artillery. Baraguey himself led the way with a couple of troopers, until fired on near Fontane. MacMahon's two divisions took the Goito road across the plain, leaving the roads along the ridge clear for I Corps. The Guard infantry marched at 5am, followed at 9am by their cavalry from Castenedolo.

Both leading corps met the enemy about 5am. Ladmirault's Division adopted the regulation attack formation to turn the flanks of the Austrian IR Nr.47: three columns forming a reversed arrowhead, each group of four battalions screened by *chasseurs*. Forey and Ladmirault pushed the Austrian outposts back from one crest to another, until they reached the ridges before Solferino. Here brigades Bils and Puchner made a stand until 10am, falling back on the cemetery and Monte di Cipressi after a prolonged and bloody resistance. Feld-Marschall-Leutnant Stadion of V Korps had prepared Solferino for defence, believing that an action was imminent. The French advance was now exposed to a cross fire from the cemetery and Monte di Cipressi, and ground to a stop. A bullet broke Ladmirault's shoulder, but he kept going until hit again, when he was forced to give up his command.

Sardinian troops assault Madonna della Scoperta as the weather closes in. Improved firearms would soon render the close-quarters fighting depicted here an anachronism. In the background is the Spia d'Italia. (Author/Bossoli)

Feldzeugmeister Benedek leads forward the Austrian IR Nr.39 at San Martino, depicted by the German artist Fritz Neumann. The red trousers of the casualty is illustrator's licence as no French troops were engaged so far north. (Author/postcard)

MacMahon had agreed with Niel that II Corps would close up on the centre, once Niel's IV Corps was securely established. Through the mist, however, MacMahon could see large columns approaching his front. These were the Austrian IX and III Korps under Schaafsgottsche and Schwarzenberg, who had yet to realize the strength of the French forces before them. Schaafsgottsche inclined left towards Medole, leaving Schwarzenberg to take the main road towards Castiglione. There was still no sign of Niel at 8.30am, when the Austrians in front of MacMahon's position appeared so threatening he deployed to receive their attack. Decaen's Division covered Casa Morino with a line of battalion columns at right angles to the main road, sheltering from Austrian artillery fire in a fold of the ground. La Motterouge's first brigade continued the line towards Medole; his second supported Decaen. Mensdorff's Kavalleriedivision could also be seen approaching from San Cassiano, outnumbering the handful of corps cavalry on MacMahon's left flank by four to one.

Schwarzenberg attacked with Schönberger's Division and 30 guns, to which MacMahon replied with his four divisional batteries. Their 24 rifled guns made short work of their opponents, knocking out several Austrian cannon and blowing up two ammunition wagons. Then Partouneaux and Desvaux arrived with their cavalry divisions, filling up the space between MacMahon's right flank and Niel's IV Corps, south of the main road. Their horse artillery advanced boldly to bring the Austrian guns under an oblique fire, forcing them to retire. An Austrian horse battery gallantly advanced to disengage the overmatched field batteries, came under fire at 1,500m, and lost five of its six guns before it could unlimber. A second battery lost three guns in a minute.

In several lucky charges, the French cavalry broke up hostile detachments infiltrating between II and IV corps, shepherding the Austrian infantry onto the French skirmishers, who made 600 of them prisoner. The Austrian cavalry were less successful against MacMahon's corps cavalry. The 7e Chasseurs à cheval drove them back upon the four leftmost French infantry battalions (11e Chasseurs and 72e Ligne), who formed square to receive Mensdorff's troopers with volleys, after which 7e Chasseurs à cheval drove them off in

TOP RIGHT

San Martino hill from the Sardinian point of view, with the monumental tower, built on the site of Roccolo Farm, half left. Contracania is half right, enfilading the attackers as they climbed the final steep slope up to the crest. (Author/photo)

BOTTOM RIGHT

The ground over which the Sardinians attacked at San Martino, seen from the tower. The Brigata Aosta advanced either side of the road on the right, their supporting artillery in front of Monata Farm. Lake Garda is in the background. (Author/photo)

disorder. MacMahon's effective combination of all three arms against superior numbers contrasts with the ill-coordinated efforts of the Austrians. Their cavalry and artillery both proved inferior to the French, while Schönberger's infantry achieved little, never coming within 180m of the French.

Leading elements of Canrobert's III Corps reinforced IV Corps (Niel) at 10.30am, freeing MacMahon to close up on the centre. He began by moving La Motterouge's Division to its left along the sunken road north of Casa Morino, behind Decaen. Once clear, La Motterouge turned half right to deploy in battalion masses covered by swarms of skirmishers, facing the village of San Cassiano, at the foot of the ridge beyond Solferino.

Baraguey's I Corps had been attacking Solferino from three sides for over an hour: Ladmirault's Division to the north on the country road from Esenta, Brigade d'Alton of Forey's Division on the heights to the west, and Brigade Dieu of the same division to the south in Pozzo Catena, also known as Pozzo di Solferino. As at Melegnano, Baraguey gave the artillery no time to prepare the attack, and his infantry were back with heavy loss. Bazaine committed his fresh division against the cemetery at 11am, but they too fell back, the fireswept ground strewn with their dead. Brigade d'Alton assaulted the Monte di Cipressi, under the eyes of the emperor, but they too were driven off. A cannonball broke the staff of the 91e Ligne's eagle, another decapitated

The narrow ridge along which the French had to approach (left), seen from the Spia d'Italia. The Castiglione road runs down the left hand wall of the cemetery and orchard (centre and right). Beyond these, gently rolling countryside stretches away towards Lake Garda. (Author/photo)

the *sous-lieutenant* who picked it up. Forey, whose white hooded cloak already sported several bullet holes, added another wound to the one he had suffered at Montebello. Napoleon himself came under fire, but refused to leave his vantage point on Monte Fenile, despite several casualties amongst his entourage and a bullet tearing off one of his own epaulettes.

Stadion had reinforced Solferino's defenders with brigades Gaal and Koller, the cemetery's high loopholed walls presenting an insuperable obstacle. It occupied the whole width of the narrow ridge along which Bazaine was trying to advance, and was constantly reinforced from the Piazza Castello. However, Stadion's supporting formation, VII Korps (Zobel), provided little help, remaining inactive towards Cavriana. Although the French attack had failed, it allowed their artillery to close the range, one battery unlimbering only 275m from the cemetery. Five battalions of Guard *voltigeurs* formed up behind Forey's Division, the *grenadiers* behind them in double company columns, the rest of the *voltigeurs* echeloned behind Forey's open right flank.

About 2pm the cemetery, Monte di Cipressi and the high ground around the Spia d'Italia were all carried together. Forey and the *voltigeurs* assailed the position's southern flank to cries of 'Vive l'Empereur', the commander of the skirmish line waving his handkerchief on his sword point, as his men swept over the Monte di Cipressi. Bazaine's 78e Ligne forced their way into the cemetery, while the rest of his division beat the *pas de charge*, and stormed the village. The outnumbered survivors of Stadion's gallant corps were in full retreat by 2.30pm, covered by Brigade Reischach of VII Korps (Zobel). Stadion's eccentric withdrawal, passing north of Cavriana, uncovered the Austrian centre, allowing the French to press on along the southern edge of the high ground. Some Guard *chasseurs* ambushed a retreating Austrian battery in Solferino's narrow village street, and drove the captured guns back through the village, meeting Napoleon on the road. Anticipating victory, he sent orders to Castiglione for the headquarters baggage wagons to set out for Cavriana, still in Austrian hands.

MacMahon's advance occurred at much the same time, La Motterouge's Division taking San Cassiano 'in a moment'. The Tirailleurs and 45e Ligne scaled Monte Fontana south-east of the village and 50m above the plain. Here

FRENCH RIFLED FIELD GUNS IN ACTION, EARLY MORNING 24 JUNE 1859 (pp. 70–71)

French rifled field guns of MacMahon's II Corps open fire across the Campo di Medole, their unprecedented accuracy stopping Austrian infantry of Schwarzenberg's III Korps dead in their tracks.

The campaign's major technological innovation was the canon de 4, rayé, modèle 1858, a traditional-style bronze muzzle-loading smoothbore gun **(1)** converted to a rifle using a system invented by two talented French officers: Ducos de la Hitte and Treuille de Beaulieu. Firing a four-kilogram segmentation shell, these weapons could engage massed targets out to three kilometres, with an effective range between 1.5 and 2.5km. The densely cultivated terrain of the early battles of the campaign had given the new guns no chance to prove themselves. The Campo di Medole, which stretches south from Solferino, however, is flat and open. Devoid of cover higher than the trampled crops of barley and rye, it provided excellent fields of fire. Pushed well forwards, French gunners took the weight of the Austrian attacks off their own outnumbered infantry, sweeping the centre of the battlefield with their fire. Once the French gun lines were established, the Austrians never came

within 180m of them, unlike Napoleonic battles where assaulting troops often overran the opposing artillery. In the distance, a ragged line of white-coated Austrian infantry stretches obliquely across the battery front, partly obscured by powder smoke **(2)**. A few Austrian victims of earlier fighting lie between the cannon **(3)**. In the foreground an Austrian rifleman has left his characteristic leather/felt Jäger hat and Model 1854 pattern carbine with its unusual broad-bladed bayonet. The nearer gun is just coming into action. While the detachment put their backs into it **(4)**, No. 1 looks towards the mounted battery commander for orders **(5)**. On the left, the next gun of the battery is reloading, surrounded by the smoke of its first round **(6)**. The gunners are wearing waist-length dark blue *vestes* and *pantalons* with white gaiters, showing they come from a field battery. All except the No. 1 have an M/1836T muzzle-loading percussion *mousqueton* or carbine, slung over the left shoulder, on top of a dark blue/grey overcoat rolled around the body. No. 1, being a senior NCO, has the old-fashioned *habit*, or tailed coat, with baggy leather-bound trousers as used by mounted troops, and an M/1829 mounted gunner's sabre in its polished steel scabbard.

they met severe resistance. The Prinz von Hesse justified his promotion after Montebello by driving the French off the hill with a series of counterattacks by IR Nr.1 and Nr.54. The 'Turcos' lost their colonel, his native Tirailleurs dipping their hands in his blood to swear vengeance. MacMahon had to wait until the Guard caught up, *grenadiers* dragging the guns up to the crest, and forming a chain to pass up ammunition from the caissons at the foot of the hill. Although the French were out of Austrian artillery range, they came under a hail of rifle fire from infantry occupying shelter trenches left over from last year's manoeuvres. The French gunners, however, soon showed the quality of their rifled guns, decimating Austrian reserves at a distance previously thought safe.

Once the Guard had linked up with II Corps, the French advanced along the heights towards Franz Josef's command post at Cavriana. The *voltigeurs* were on the left, in line with MacMahon's divisions: La Motterouge on the hill slopes of Monte Fontana, Decaen on the plain below. Forey's battered division and a brigade of *grenadiers* followed, while Bazaine pursued Stadion's V Korps towards Pozzolengo. Ladmirault's sorely tried division remained at Solferino. On the far right the Guard cavalry (Morris) guarded Decaen's exposed right flank. Parts of Austrian I, V and VII Korps opposed the advance, but they had no time to regroup, and neither Clam Gallas's nor Zobel's Korps had recovered from Magenta. Clam Gallas had mislaid his reserve artillery, and the staff officer sent to find it was unhorsed, wandering the battlefield on foot. Decaen overthrew Brigade Brunner of I Korps, while the Guard cavalry drove off a final charge by Mensdorff's reserve cavalry.

The Prinz von Hesse gave up his gallant attempts to stem the Austrian collapse about 3.30pm, evacuating Cavriana an hour before the French arrived. Franz Josef rode back through Volta about 5pm, weeping tears of impotent fury at his troops' refusal to stand. His cousin, the Duca di Modena, was reported foaming at the mouth with vexation. In the confusion the Imperial staff came within half a mile of a French brigade, who might have

An attackers' view of the approaches to Solferino, showing the Austrians' mutually supporting positions in the Piazza Castello (left) and on Monte di Cipressi (right). Note the obstacle posed by vineyards to troops wishing to move across rather than along the rows of plants. (Author/photo)

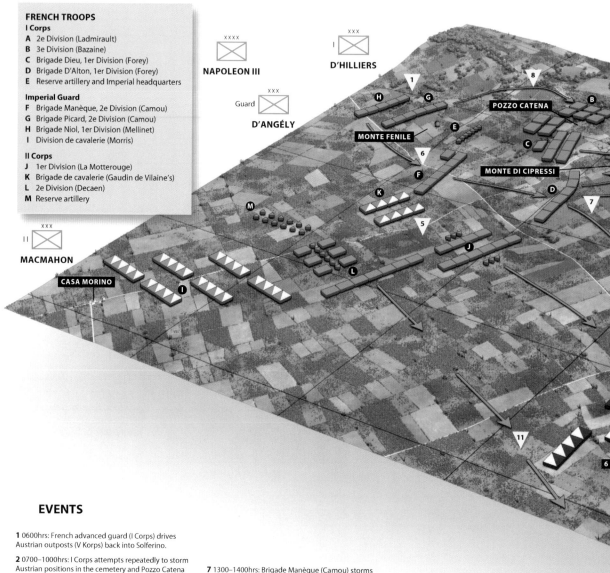

FRENCH TROOPS

I Corps
A 2e Division (Ladmirault)
B 3e Division (Bazaine)
C Brigade Dieu, 1er Division (Forey)
D Brigade D'Alton, 1er Division (Forey)
E Reserve artillery and Imperial headquarters

Imperial Guard
F Brigade Manèque, 2e Division (Camou)
G Brigade Picard, 2e Division (Camou)
H Brigade Niol, 1er Division (Mellinet)
I Division de cavalerie (Morris)

II Corps
J 1er Division (La Motterouge)
K Brigade de cavalerie (Gaudin de Vilaine's)
L 2e Division (Decaen)
M Reserve artillery

NAPOLEON III

D'HILLIERS

Guard

D'ANGÉLY

MACMAHON

CASA MORINO

POZZO CATENA

MONTE FENILE

MONTE DI CIPRESSI

EVENTS

1 0600hrs: French advanced guard (I Corps) drives Austrian outposts (V Korps) back into Solferino.

2 0700–1000hrs: I Corps attempts repeatedly to storm Austrian positions in the cemetery and Pozzo Catena without success, using up all but one of its brigades.

3 1100hrs: Napoleon commits Brigade D'Alton of Forey's Division against Monte di Cipressi, hoping to unlock the centre. The attack fails with heavy loss.

4 Despite the French failure to break through, two Austrian brigades (V Korps) leave the action. More Austrian units (from I Korps) join Solferino's defenders, leaving San Cassiano thinly defended.

5 Meanwhile MacMahon's II Corps closes up from Casa Morino onto the right flank of I Corps, wheeling right to face San Cassiano. The Guard cavalry under Morris fill the gap created on MacMahon's own right flank.

6 1100–1200hrs: Camou's Division of *voltigeurs* (Guard), followed by Mellinet's *grenadiers*, deploys behind the exhausted I Corps.

7 1300–1400hrs: Brigade Manèque (Camou) storms Monte di Cipressi and Monte Roccolo, supported by Forey, cutting off the defenders of the cemetery.

8 Brigade Picard moves left and forward to support I Corps.

9 1400hrs: Bazaine's Division storms the now-isolated cemetery, and breaks into Solferino, whose defenders retreat north-eastwards.

10 1430hrs: La Motterouge's Division (II Corps) assaults San Cassiano with ten battalions against five. Pushing on to Monte Fontana, they tear a huge hole in the enemy line. Austrian headquarters at Cavriana withdraws under shellfire.

11 Decaen's Division (II Corps), followed by the Guard cavalry, moves up to consolidate La Motterouge's open left flank.

FRENCH BREAKTHROUGH AT SOLFERINO

Just after midday, the French Imperial Guard broke through the Austrian centre. Turning the high ground at Spia d'Italia, they cleared the way for I Corps to storm Solferino, after repeated assaults, while II Corps advanced on San Cassiano, threatening Austrian headquarters at Cavriana.

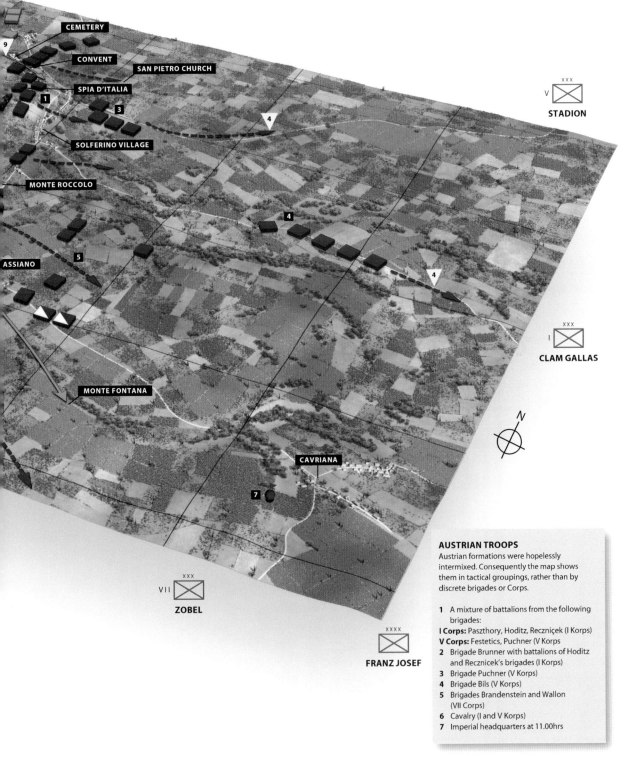

CEMETERY

9

CONVENT

SAN PIETRO CHURCH

SPIA D'ITALIA

1

3

SOLFERINO VILLAGE

MONTE ROCCOLO

ASSIANO

5

MONTE FONTANA

CAVRIANA

7

4

STADION

XXX
V

4

4

CLAM GALLAS
XXX
I

N

ZOBEL
XXX
VII

FRANZ JOSEF
XXXX

AUSTRIAN TROOPS
Austrian formations were hopelessly
intermixed. Consequently the map shows
them in tactical groupings, rather than by
discrete brigades or Corps.

1   A mixture of battalions from the following
    brigades:
I Corps: Paszthory, Hoditz, Reczniçek (I Korps)
V Corps: Festetics, Puchner (V Korps
2   Brigade Brunner with battalions of Hoditz
    and Recznicek's brigades (I Korps)
3   Brigade Puchner (V Korps)
4   Brigade Bils (V Korps)
5   Brigades Brandenstein and Wallon
    (VII Corps)
6   Cavalry (I and V Korps)
7   Imperial headquarters at 11.00hrs

75

wiped out the whole lot with a few well-aimed volleys. The French attempted little pursuit after the pouring rain that followed. Two batteries of horse artillery, however, continued to shell the retiring Austrians from the hills around Cavriana, converting an orderly retreat into a regular *sauve qui peut*. That night Napoleon III slept at the Villa Mirra-Siliprandi in Cavriana, in the bed prepared for Franz Josef.

French losses in the centre totalled: 1,025 killed, 4,852 wounded and 997 missing. Austrian Zweite Armee lost 9,326, excluding VIII Korps (Benedek). Over 4,000 French casualties came from I Corps (Baraguey), more than a sixth of their strength. Half the Austrian casualties came from V Korps (Stadion), which with the 1,500 Austrian prisoners taken in Solferino suggests the intensity of the fighting there.

THE SOUTHERN FLANK

The Allied right, consisting of III and IV corps (Canrobert and Niel), had encamped either side of the Chiese near Carpenedolo. Both were powerful formations with three infantry divisions each. They played very different parts in the battle.

Canrobert's Corps was further to the rear, all its divisions having to cross the Chiese. They set out at 2.30am, passing the river on a bridge put up by Sardinian engineers at Visano. Renault's Division led the way, followed by Trochu and then Bourbaki, forming a column 11km long. They cleared some Austrian hussars out of Castel Goffredo about 7am, and approached Medole at 9.15am, where Canrobert received urgent calls for help from Niel, who was already in action towards Guidizzolo. At the same time two staff officers arrived from Napoleon with contradictory instructions. Canrobert was to support Niel, while simultaneously looking out for 25,000 Austrians reported to have left Mantua the previous day. He had already detached his own cavalry division (Partouneaux) to support IV Corps, and was unable to mount an effective reconnaissance. However, the *maréchal* could see clouds of dust to the south, which local people confirmed to be Austrian troop movements.

Canrobert, therefore, limited his initial support for Niel to just half of Renault's Division, sent after de Luzy's Division along the bank of the Seriola Marchionale. Arriving at 10.30pm, Brigade Jannin gave Niel sufficient

Chasseurs of Brigade Manèque of the Guard advance on Monte Alto, leaving the Spia d'Italia and Monte di Cipressi to their left, and opening the way for MacMahon's Corps to storm through the Austrian centre on their right. Solferino village is visible between the hills. (Author/INW)

confidence to dispense with MacMahon, freeing II Corps to join the attack on the Austrian centre at San Cassiano. Not until 3pm did Canrobert feel it safe to send all of Renault's Division to strengthen Niel's line at Rebecco. Brigade Bataille of Trochu's Division followed an hour later, coming into reserve between Casa Nova and Báite. At last, far too late to be useful, Canrobert released Bourbaki's Division, just leaving Trochu's other brigade (Collineau) to watch the southern flank. Canrobert personally was the bravest of men. He had once bluffed his way through a mass of hostile Arabs in Algeria by telling them his regiment carried the plague in its ranks. Responsibility, however, seemed to paralyze him. During his period as French commander-in-chief in the Crimea, his frustrated British allies had known him as Robert Can't.

Meanwhile Niel was fighting for his life. De Luzy's Division had led the way, preceded by Rochefort's *chasseurs à cheval*. Vinoy's Division followed, then the corps artillery and de Failly's Division last. The troops moved slowly, restricted to the road by waist-deep irrigation ditches. Reports suggested that Austrian troops sighted at Medole had retreated as usual. However, ten companies of IR Nr.52 were still in possession, supported by six squadrons of FML Zedtwitz's Kavalleriedivision (Brigade Vopaterny). De Luzy shelled the infantry out of the village while sending columns to turn its flanks. A lucky shell brought down the church bell on some Austrians using the tower as an observation post, and the surviving Austrian infantry retired on Rebecco at 7am. Brigade Douay went after them, three more of de Luzy's battalions following the Austrian cavalry towards Ceresara.

Here Zedtwitz expected to find the rest of his division, but the brigade commander (Lauingen) had decided the ground was unsuitable for cavalry, so he withdrew to Goito, while regimental officers broke their swords and wept with rage. Zedtwitz followed, depriving the Austrian left wing of its reserve cavalry for the rest of the day. The horses had eaten nothing for 36 hours, and were exhausted, but what sort of cavalry leader allows his horses to starve in one of the most fertile regions of Europe?

When Niel's infantry emerged from Medole, they met strong Austrian columns from IX Korps (Schaafsgottsche) and III Korps (Schwarzenberg), who were also engaged with MacMahon at Casa Morino. During the morning four of the five brigades of XI Korps (Weigl) arrived from Castel Grimaldo. Niel's

Général Niel whose epic stand on the French right earned him immediate promotion to *maréchal*. An engineer officer who had served at Sebastopol in 1855, his decorations included the British Order of the Bath and an Ottoman medal. (RNM/ILN)

Another view of the decisive moment of the battle, showing the astonishing depth of the French assault formations, although the artist has mistakenly put the high ground on the right flank. The troops in shakoes (right) are Guard *voltigeurs*. (Author/lemonde)

77

AUSTRIAN CAVALRY CHARGE, AFTERNOON 24 JUNE 1859 (pp. 78–79)

Austrian Husarenregiment Nr.10 seeks in vain to halt the French advance after the fall of Solferino. Cavalry's inability to break rifle-armed infantry in 1859 anticipated a reduced role for mounted troops on European and American battlefields. Neither side's cavalry at Solferino were able to take advantage of the opportunities offered them by the open ground in the southern part of the battlefield.

Four ranks deep to receive cavalry, French line infantry (1) have just opened fire from the edge of a cornfield. Normally the front two ranks of a square would kneel down with their bayonets pointing outwards, while the rear two took turns to fire and reload. Here the front ranks have stood up to fire a volley at close range, to inflict maximum damage. Meanwhile the rear ranks are reloading as fast as they can, biting tops off cartridges and ramming them down, in case a second wave of cavalry arrives (2). The men are in regulation campaign dress: crimson kepi; iron grey/blue overcoat with skirts buttoned back clear of legs and crimson epaulettes showing they are from a grenadier company; dark red woollen trousers; black canvas gaiters obscured by dust and trampled corn. Firearms are M/1853 rifled percussion muskets with triangular socket bayonets. Infantry rifles lacked sights, but were deadly at ranges as close as this.

Two hussars are down already (3), and the trumpeter has just been hit (4) behind an officer recognizable from his gold embroidered shoulder belt. Ignoring his shouted encouragement, the nearest two troopers have reined in, one of them firing his Model 1850 smoothbore single shot percussion pistol as he turns away (5).

Austrian hussars wore a tightly waisted tunic, or *Attila*, under a *pelisse* trimmed with black lambswool. Regimental shades varied: in this case light blue with yellow/black frogging. The *pelisse* was slung over the left shoulder, flying about with the rider's motion. Concessions to active service include green oilcloth shako covers, and Russian-grey overall trousers, the soft black leather reinforcements below the knee looking misleadingly like long boots.

Sidearms are the Model 1850 standard Austrian cavalry sabre with a more elaborate hilt and gold sword knot for officers. The sabretache, or flat message case hanging from the steel scabbard, bears the imperial cypher, an entwined F and J for Franz Josef (6). The regimental standard (7) features more Imperial heraldry: a double-headed eagle with the emperor's coat of arms on its breast.

Casa Nova from the south, looking along Niel's front line from the road past Báite. The flat open terrain is typical of the battlefield's southern sector, the only cover provided by farm buildings and their surrounding trees. (Author/photo)

six brigades had, therefore, to deal with up to 12 Austrian ones, more than twice their nominal strength. Nevertheless, the French gradually drove back their opponents. De Luzy's Division was committed towards Ceresara and Rebecco, so Vinoy was sent to the left, with 6e Chasseurs à pied skirmishing through the thickets to take an isolated farm called Casa Nova. Situated between the more densely cultivated ground and the open plain to the south-east, Casa Nova would be the scene of desperate fighting all day.

The ground here was open enough for Niel to make out MacMahon's II Corps at Casa Morino, so he threw back Vinoy's left flank, to join up with them. When MacMahon's Corps advanced on San Cassiano, Vinoy brought up his left flank, taking another farmhouse at Quagliara, 100m north of Casa Nova. Niel reinforced Vinoy's divisional batteries with the corps artillery reserve, filling the 2,800m gap between his own left and MacMahon's right flank with a Napoleonic grand battery supported on its left by Partouneaux's and Desvaux's cavalry divisions. Austrian troops tried to exploit the gap between the French corps, but the 42 rifled guns in action north of Quagliara soon checked their advance. De Luzy's Division defended Rebecco against the whole of IX Korps (Schaafsgottsche), the latter reinforced by brigades Baltin and Blomberg of XI Korps (Weigl). One of de Failly's brigades (O'Farrell) held the hamlet of Báite to connect Vinoy and de Luzy. The other (Saurin) remained at Medole, to be fed gradually into the firing line. Beyond Niel's right, Brigade Jannin of III Corps provided a solid support on the Ceresara road along the Seriola Marchionale, threatening the left flank of Austrian columns swinging south of Rebecco from Guidizzolo.

Fortunately for the French, Schaafsgottsche had not seen the need for any special measures to recover Medole, and failed to coordinate the movements of his five brigades. At this point the plain was still much enclosed, and Austrian brigades wandered about, coming into action piecemeal. Crenneville's two brigades (Blumencron and Fehlmayer) on Schaafsgottsche's right were threatened on one flank by MacMahon, and fired into by Vinoy on the other. Further south the three brigades of Handl's Division came up separately, and found the French ready for them. At 9am the remains of Crenneville's Division stood on the main Mantua–Castiglione road confronting Vinoy between Medole and Guidizzolo. Two of Handl's brigades were engaged with de Luzy's Division at Rebecco, while the other had fallen back shattered upon Guidizzolo.

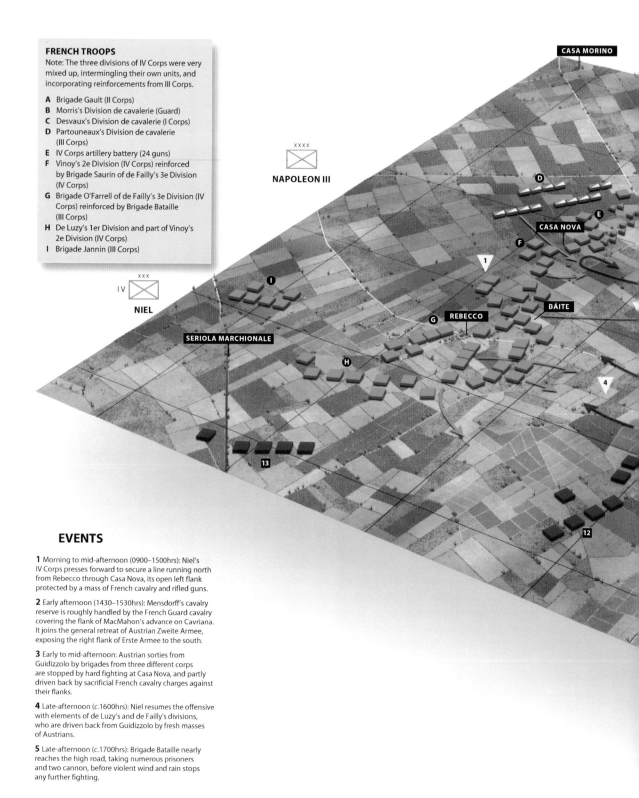

FRENCH TROOPS
Note: The three divisions of IV Corps were very mixed up, intermingling their own units, and incorporating reinforcements from III Corps.

A Brigade Gault (II Corps)
B Morris's Division de cavalerie (Guard)
C Desvaux's Division de cavalerie (I Corps)
D Partouneaux's Division de cavalerie (III Corps)
E IV Corps artillery battery (24 guns)
F Vinoy's 2e Division (IV Corps) reinforced by Brigade Saurin of de Failly's 3e Division (IV Corps)
G Brigade O'Farrell of de Failly's 3e Division (IV Corps) reinforced by Brigade Bataille (III Corps)
H De Luzy's 1er Division and part of Vinoy's 2e Division (IV Corps)
I Brigade Jannin (III Corps)

XXXX

NAPOLEON III

XXX
I V
NIEL

CASA MORINO

CASA NOVA

DÁITE

REBECCO

SERIOLA MARCHIONALE

EVENTS

1 Morning to mid-afternoon (0900–1500hrs): Niel's IV Corps presses forward to secure a line running north from Rebecco through Casa Nova, its open left flank protected by a mass of French cavalry and rifled guns.

2 Early afternoon (1430–1530hrs): Mensdorff's cavalry reserve is roughly handled by the French Guard cavalry covering the flank of MacMahon's advance on Cavriana. It joins the general retreat of Austrian Zweite Armee, exposing the right flank of Erste Armee to the south.

3 Early to mid-afternoon: Austrian sorties from Guidizzolo by brigades from three different corps are stopped by hard fighting at Casa Nova, and partly driven back by sacrificial French cavalry charges against their flanks.

4 Late-afternoon (c.1600hrs): Niel resumes the offensive with elements of de Luzy's and de Failly's divisions, who are driven back from Guidizzolo by fresh masses of Austrians.

5 Late-afternoon (c.1700hrs): Brigade Bataille nearly reaches the high road, taking numerous prisoners and two cannon, before violent wind and rain stops any further fighting.

THE FRENCH STAND ON THE CAMPO DI MEDOLE

The overwhelming French concentration at Solferino left their southern corps outnumbered two to one. Despite their numerical disadvantage, the French held their ground throughout the day, and even launched their own counter-offensive, shortly before the storm that ended the battle at 5pm.

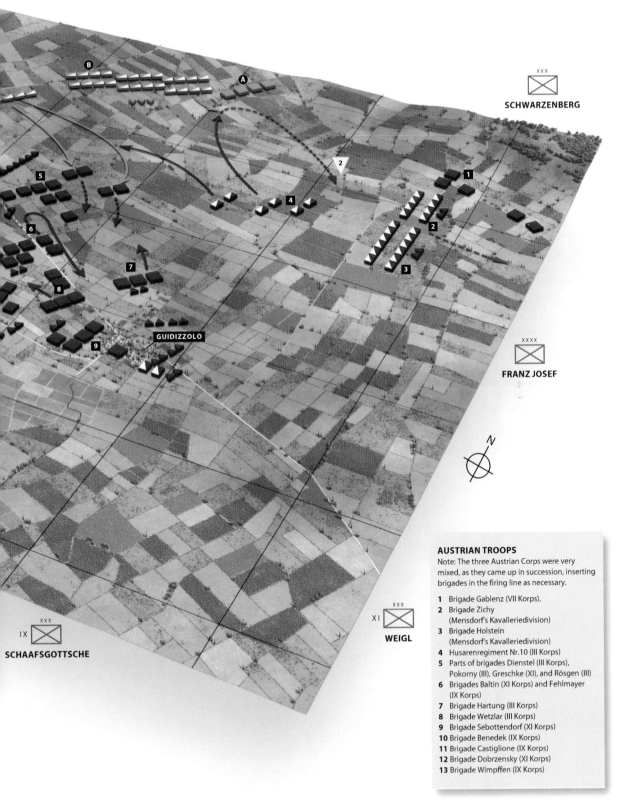

Note: Gridlines are shown at intervals of 1km/1093yds

SCHWARZENBERG

FRANZ JOSEF

GUIDIZZOLO

SCHAAFSGOTTSCHE

WEIGL

AUSTRIAN TROOPS

Note: The three Austrian Corps were very mixed, as they came up in succession, inserting brigades in the firing line as necessary.

1　Brigade Gablenz (VII Korps).
2　Brigade Zichy
　　(Mensdorf's Kavalleriedivision)
3　Brigade Holstein
　　(Mensdorf's Kavalleriedivision)
4　Husarenregiment Nr.10 (III Korps)
5　Parts of brigades Dienstel (III Korps),
　　Pokorny (III), Greschke (XI), and Rösgen (III)
6　Brigades Baltin (XI Korps) and Fehlmayer
　　(IX Korps)
7　Brigade Hartung (III Korps)
8　Brigade Wetzlar (III Korps)
9　Brigade Sebottendorf (XI Korps)
10　Brigade Benedek (IX Korps)
11　Brigade Castiglione (IX Korps)
12　Brigade Dobrzensky (XI Korps)
13　Brigade Wimpffen (IX Korps)

Généraux Niel and Vinoy organize the defence of Quagliara Farm, on the right flank of the great battery that protected the French centre. The slight rise is artist's licence, probably to show the Austrian masses through the smoke. The ground here is utterly flat. (RNM/ILN)

Fighting continued over much the same ground for another six hours. On the left, where his artillery played the major part, Niel wrote afterwards that the French, 'had always an incontestable superiority'. Elsewhere, he reported, the struggle was less one-sided: 'When the combat was carried on by the fire of the infantry, I lost ground, the enemy having the advantage in numbers. Then I formed a column of attack with one of my reserve battalions, and gained more by the bayonet than I had lost by the musketry.'

The fighting was often desperate. Some Austrian infantry soldiers fired 180 rounds apiece, three times the contents of their pouches, and an astonishing expenditure of ammunition for the time. In Niel's centre at Báite, 2e Ligne nearly lost its eagle, all six company commanders of its third battalion becoming casualties. A little to the north, Colonel Maleville of 55e Ligne was shot down at the head of his men, holding aloft the regimental colours. By mid-afternoon, the French were exhausted after 12 hours' continuous marching and fighting in a waterless country where the stifling heat anticipated the storm about to burst. Austrian rockets and case shot swept the Casa Nova, rendering its continued occupation almost impossible. Uhlans and massed infantry assailed 6e Chasseurs, who shot Colonel Windischgrätz of IR Nr.35 off his horse underneath the very walls of the farm. Général de Clérambault led forward the *hussard* brigade of Partouneaux's Division to gain the defenders a brief respite. Unable to see more than a few yards ahead, he found himself on the flank of a Croat battalion. The *Grenzer* lay down to avoid the charge, springing up to fire when the first wave of cavalry had passed, only to be swept away by the supporting squadrons.

Renault's Division from III Corps (Canrobert) closed up behind Rebecco about 3pm, allowing Niel to launch an attack on Guidizzolo with six battalions drawn from de Luzy's and de Failly's divisions. They reached the first houses of the village but met fresh masses of Austrian troops, collected for a last-ditch attempt to restore the situation in the centre, and fell back. Franz Josef would not accept that Stadion's defeat meant the battle was over, despite the loss of Solferino, the pivot around which the whole Austrian plan revolved. He ordered FZM Graf Wimpffen, commander of Erste Armee, to make a final effort to drive the Allies northwards into Lake Garda. His infantry, exhausted in ill-coordinated defensive fighting on empty stomachs, and his cavalry vanished, Wimpffen was not the man to save the day. Known as the 'begging friar' from his unfortunate appearance on horseback, the Austrian commander was already considering retreat when Niel's over-optimistic offensive disrupted his halfhearted preparations to execute Franz Josef's instructions.

Meanwhile, Canrobert had verified the situation beyond his right flank, finding no sign of the, 'mythical men of Mantua'. Liechtenstein's halfhearted turning movement had petered out at Marcaria, alarmed by reports of the arrival of d'Autemarre's Division of V Corps (Prince Napoleon) from Tuscany. Canrobert immediately released Brigade Bataille of Trochu's Division, and promised Bourbaki's Division by nightfall. He had been unlucky to receive the emperor's directions when he did. Otherwise he might have come to the aid of IV Corps much sooner, in a more decisive fashion.

Now Bataille's advance was held up by convoys of wounded soldiers from IV Corps. Arriving at Rebecco, Trochu deployed the brigade's battalions just south of Casa Nova in close columns of companies, *en échiquier* or chequerboard fashion, and led them to the assault as coolly as on the parade ground. Desvaux's cavalry division moved up on Bataille's left, meeting a column of Hungarian infantry amidst the vineyards and thickets. Despite the unfavourable ground, Desvaux prepared to charge, forming his division in two lines, the 5e Hussards and 1er Chasseurs d'Afrique in front supported by 3e Chasseurs d'Afrique. The 1er Chasseurs cut down the Hungarian skirmishers, driving them back onto the troops they were meant to cover, and breaking a half-formed square. The other Austrian battalions were less impressed, firing volleys and bayoneting any individual cavalrymen unlucky enough to break into their ranks. The leading *chasseur* regiment lost its colonel and ten other officers in two futile charges, before the surviving troopers fell back on their supports.

Colonel Maleville of the 55e Ligne shot from his horse near Báite, leading a bayonet charge after his regiment had expended all its ammunition. For once, the opposing troops may have been as close together as the artist suggests. (Author/ILN)

Bataille's leading infantry had not reached Guidizzolo, when the storm that had been threatening all day finally broke, preceded by whirlwinds of yellow dust, mistaken at first for an Austrian cavalry attack. The ensuing downpour plunged the battlefield into darkness, bringing the epic struggle to an end. Erste Armee took the opportunity to escape, its corps retiring as follows:

Corps	Retreat
III (Schwarzenberg)	by Cerlungo to Ferri
IX (Schaafsgottsche)	to Goito
XI (Weigl)	by Goito to Roverbella

Weigl covered the retreat, remaining in Guidizzolo until late in the evening. Erste Armee's losses totalled 9,796. French losses on the right were:

	Killed	Wounded	Missing
III Corps (Canrobert)	37	257	19
IV Corps (Niel)	552	3,552	501
Partouneaux's Division	13	51	4
Desvaux's Division	58	152	42
TOTALS	660	4,012	566

Niel's losses were in proportion to his share of the fighting. In recompense, his corps claimed numerous trophies: the colours of IR Nr.35, seven guns and 2,000 prisoners.

AFTER THE BATTLE

The Allies were in no state to pursue, after up to 18 hours of marching and fighting. Austrian rearguards held Guidizzolo and Volta until 10pm on the night of the battle, the beaten army recrossing the Mincio unmolested. Total Allied losses were about 17,000, compared with up to 22,000 Austrians, but the moral effect of the latters' defeat was far greater than casualties alone might suggest. Every corps of the Austrian Army had been defeated in a battle that its leaders had deliberately sought, with the intention of provoking a decision. Three days after the battle Franz Josef's army commanders still thought their troops would not stand if attacked. That night, 27/28 June, they fell back on the river Adige, leaving garrisons at Mantua and Peschiera.

The main causes of the Austrian defeat were as follows:

1) Lack of a central reserve: when the Kaiser issued orders directly to individual corps, he found them already committed; left to themselves, the Army commanders did nothing.

2) Poor offensive spirit: the troops took up defensive positions as soon as they met the enemy, although they were meant to be attacking. A senior Austrian officer commented: 'Our brave infantry fellows have not the dash or quickness of the French; they stood up to be shot at.'

3) Solferino's faults as a defensive position: protecting only an eighth of the Austrian front, its steep and narrow ridges prevented close-range defensive artillery fire, while poor access from the village to the cemetery hindered insertion of reserves.

French troops crossing the Mincio, the towers of Valeggio in the background: three days after the battle, the Austrian troops were still too demoralized for their commanders to risk another battle to defend the river. (Author/ILN)

The Times credited the French victory to their skill at skirmishing, but the similar numbers of killed and wounded on the two sides do not support this. A more significant factor may have been the crops, which denied defending riflemen a clear field of fire. Higher losses among French gunners, compared with Magenta, suggest that rifled guns played a more prominent role in the final battle. Général Auger was mortally wounded directing the fire of MacMahon's batteries in the centre. Niel commented on the undeniable advantage enjoyed by his artillery, its terrible effects shown by the fragments of men and horses that littered the ground. Both sides claimed to have fought heroically against superior numbers. In fact, losses of one-twelfth to one-eighth threw the Austrians into hopeless disorder, and prevented them from risking action three days later. By comparison the British lost almost a third of their numbers at Inkerman (1854), the victors at Gettysburg (1863) a fifth. While the French upheld their reputation for dashing attacks, the Austrian infantry were quite unable to hold their ground against them. Far less were they able to redeem the mistakes of their generals, who had won the battle of Solferino every previous year in exercises, but were beaten the first time they fought it for real. It was rather as if an invader were to rout the British Army on Salisbury Plain.

Allied siege operations began promptly against Peschiera, the northern fortress of the Quadrilateral. The Sardinians completed their investment by 1 July, covered by the French who crossed the Mincio further south. Engineer officers examined Peschiera's defences from balloons, and estimated that Verona might hold out for three or four months, an unwelcome reminder of the protracted siege of Sebastopol during the Crimean War. Rifled siege guns were brought up by rail from France, and prefabricated gunboats assembled on Lake Garda.

The war was about to enter a more serious phase. The Allies formed a Hungarian legion from prisoners of war, threatening the stability of the Habsburg Empire, and moved a large fleet on Venice in the Austrian rear. Austrian reinforcements arrived in the shape of fifth battalions and volunteer corps. More alarmingly for the French, Prussia mobilized 132,000 troops on France's north-east border along the Rhine, as war fever swept across

Both sides mobilized fresh forces after Solferino: here Hungarian volunteers leave home to join Habsburg forces in Italy. Meanwhile, the Allies were recruiting disaffected Hungarian prisoners of war to fight for them. (Author/ILN)

Two emperors meet on the road to Villafranca to agree an armistice, sidelining the king of Sardinia. The peace terms outraged Italian nationalists, but Solferino had created a momentum towards unity that could not be denied. (Author/Bossoli)

Germany. Napoleon was willing, therefore, to exploit the diplomatic opening provided by enquiries after Fürst Windischgrätz, who had been killed at Casa Nova. On 6 July Comte Fleury, one of Napoleon's closest confederates, travelled melodramatically to Verona in a coach with drawn blinds. Overnight he agreed an armistice with Franz Josef, confirmed two days later in a personal interview between the two emperors at Villafranca. Sardinia gained Lombardy, but Venice would remain in Austrian hands. For the time being Sardinia retained Nice and Savoy.

The latest twist in French diplomacy outraged Italian patriots, but Magenta and Solferino had started a process that could not be reversed. Never again would Austrian troops intervene to prop up unpopular Italian regimes. The next year saw the famous expedition of Garibaldi's 'Thousand' to Sicily, and by 1870 the whole of Italy would be united under Vittorio Emmanuele.

The Italian campaign provided few clear lessons. Improved weapons technology might have been expected to cause prolonged firefights, but after Montebello the bayonet was in fashion among the Allies. Far from commanding their troops, French officers had to obey their cries of 'à la baionette', and follow their 'fuite en avant' towards the enemy. Participants and critics were equally confused. Napoleon III knew how slender his margin of victory had been, urging senior officers at a victory banquet to address the problems revealed in Italy. The apparent ease of their success, however, fed a disastrous complacency, confirming French soldiers and politicians in their belief that an effective army required neither proper funding nor systematic preparation for war. The Austrian Army was supposed to be second only to the French, while the Prussian Army was considered no better than a militia. French victories at Magenta and Solferino were significant contributory factors in their defeats at the hands of the latter during the Franco-Prussian War of 1870–71.

The Austrians drew entirely wrong conclusions from their failure to halt French bayonet attacks by rifle fire. They abandoned musketry training completely, teaching troops to leave advantageous defensive positions and storm forwards with the bayonet. This tactical lunacy, known as *Stosstaktik*, resulted in stiff casualties against the Danish Army in 1864, and disaster against Prussian breech-loading rifles in 1866. Fundamental weaknesses in

the command structure were never addressed, although Grünne had to resign, as did Hess, worn out by age and disappointment. A few prominent examples were made. The cavalry general who led his brigade off the field at Solferino was confined to a fortress, and his divisional commander cashiered. Benedek, the hero of San Martino, replaced Hess as Chief of the Quarter-Master's Staff, but showed more interest in preserving the old army spirit than professionalizing the officer corps. Hess commented to Fleury at Verona, 'Your rifled guns cut our reserves to pieces', and the Austrians did rearm their artillery, which became the most effective part of the Habsburg forces.

Critics found little new in the Italian campaign. Napoleon III had apparently done nothing his uncle might not have done, although modern technology helped him do it quicker. The telegraph allowed both sides' heads of government to control operations from a distance, several commentators blaming counter-orders from Vienna for the failure of Gyulai's offensive. News of victory and peace travelled with unprecedented rapidity, making public opinion more important than before. The French Army had its own telegraphy section, and even a mobile printing press. Its use of railways under the enemy's very nose was dismissed as a hazardous curiosity, however. Railways had to wait until the American Civil War to be recognized as a new military arm.

Their most significant achievement in 1859 may have been casualty evacuation. There was no time to convert rolling stock into ambulances, but the rapid dispersal of wounded to the rear by rail forestalled the epidemics that usually decimated front-line hospitals. Nevertheless, the human cost of the battle so horrified Henri Dunant, a passing Swiss businessman, that he went on to convene the 1863 Geneva Conference, from which emerged the International Red Cross and the Geneva Convention of 1864. Between them these are the most significant steps yet taken towards ameliorating the horrors of war, and they remain Solferino's best-known consequence.

The tactics employed at Solferino seemed to show that existing formations and even cavalry could adapt to the new weapons, a conclusion at odds with the ragged firing lines and trench warfare of the American Civil War, a few years later. More suggestive of future trends was the limited effect of long-range artillery. Too exposed if placed forward on the flanks, it was unable to see its targets if held back. If Solferino failed to teach any new truths, it did illustrate some old ones: the result of a battle may depend on an accidental feature of the ground; troops should be brought into action in masses not in penny packets; if they are to be of any use, they must be properly fed and equipped.

THE BATTLEFIELDS TODAY

The battlefields of 1859 are relatively unchanged and worth visiting, particularly Solferino and San Martino. The Touring Club Italiano's 1:200,000 map of Lombardy (ISBN 88-365-0219-9) marks them all with the usual crossed swords symbol. The Istituto Geografico Militare's 1:50,000 maps are less helpful. Individual sheets are small (25km square), expensive (£14 at time of writing), and out of date. They do not mark battlefields, and may not name features mentioned in the text. They should be obtained before leaving for Italy. Map sheets and grid references appear below where available. Northern Italian weather is variable, and visitors should be ready for extremes of rain and sun.

Montebello (no 1:50,000 map)
Montebello lies 24km south of Pavia, whence the main road (No. 35) crosses the Po, and follows the route of brigades Gaal and Bils past Casatisma to Casteggio. From there take the Voghera road (No. 10), and Montebello is on the left. It remains a hilltop village, with views across flatter parts of the battlefield to the north-west. Near Montebello church, at the highest point of the village, is a statue of a Sardinian cavalryman, commemorating their role in the battle. The road down through the north end of the village passes the

The entrance to the Piazza Castello today, with one of several storyboards set up around Solferino to interpret key points of the battle. The building on the left still appears to show the scars. (Author/photo)

cemetery where Général Beuret was killed. An ossuary on the Voghera road contains the bones of men killed in the action, and further west an Austrian cannonball remains embedded in the church wall at Genestrello.

Palestro (no 1:50,000 map)
The battlefield is ten kilometres east of Vercelli along the Mortara road (No. 596). Country roads connect the scenes of action at Palestro, Vinzaglio and Confienza. The Austrian disaster at Ponte Brida took place two kilometres south of Palestro. There is a monument in the middle of Palestro village, surmounted by a Sardinian infantryman and an ossuary on the outskirts.

Magenta (IGM sheet 117 Legnano)
Magenta lies 24km west of Milan, from where it can be reached by the Novara road (No. 11), or intermittently by rail from Stazione Porta Garibaldi. Ponte Vecchio (MR8933) and Boffalora (MR8635), the northern and southern limits of the fighting on the Naviglio Grande, are within walking distance of Magenta station three to four kilometres. A towpath runs past Ponte Nuovo (MR8834), where the customs houses still stand beside a very busy main road. Unfortunately, factories obscure the ground between Boffalora and Magenta, and two dual carriageways cross the road taken by La Motterouge's Division past Cascina Nuova (MR8835) into Magenta, making the walk hazardous. Marcallo and Mesero have both expanded, obscuring the countryside through which Espinasse approached. The local authorities, however, have erected signboards around Magenta, pinpointing places of interest: monuments near the station, the house where Général Espinasse was killed, the market place and cemetery where the Austrians held out to the end. An illustrated *Guida-Itinerario* is available in Italian, French and German, from Commune di Magenta, Piazza Formenti, 3.

Solferino (IGM sheet 143 Castiglione delle Stiviere)
The French sector of the battlefield is 12km south-east of Lake Garda, and extends eight kilometres southwards. It is not accessible by public transport. Within this large area lie the following areas of interest:

a) Solferino village (PR2225), the decisive point of the battle. Take the main Goito road from Castiglione (No. 236), turning left at Casa Morino, past an unmarked commemorative obelisk. Follow a minor road north along the line occupied by MacMahon's II Corps. Bear right below the Spia d'Italia into Solferino to see:

- The ossuary north of the village, in the old parish church of St Peter. Restored since the battle, it contains over 7,000 skeletons.

- The museum between the ossuary and village, containing numerous relics of the battle. Closed Mondays, it has a website at www.solferinoesanmartino.it, showing opening times and admission charges for itself and its associated museum at San Martino.

- The Spia d'Italia on the hilltop west of the village: a 23m-high medieval tower containing relics of the battle, including French and Sardinian cannon. If you go nowhere else, climb to the top for a panoramic view of the whole battlefield, including the Monte di Cipressi.

- The Piazza Castello, north-west of the Spia, including the convent church of San Nicola. The cemetery stormed by Bazaine's Division is 300m further west. It has been extended and rebuilt, obscuring any features contemporary with the battle. However, a track along the ridge to the west provides excellent views of Pozzo Catena, the Piazza Castello and Spia d'Italia from the French point of view.

b) Cavriana (MR2523) is 4.3km east of Solferino, past Monte Fontana, which was stormed by MacMahon's Turcos. Villa Mirra-Siliprandi, where the two emperors slept before and after the battle, now houses an archaeological museum. The road south to Guidizzolo runs along the front of Mensdorff's Austrian reserve cavalry (PR2521).

c) Fürst Windischgrätz's monument at Casa Nova (PR2120) set back from the quiet minor road north of Rebecco, which was the front line of Niel's IV Corps for much of the day. The Seriola Marchionale beyond Rebecco (PR2117) marks the southern edge of the fighting. Do not confuse it with a modern irrigation canal within the village.

d) Castiglione delle Stiviere (PR1627) housed both sides' wounded after Solferino, and has a museum devoted to the Red Cross, in the old Triulzi-Longhi Palace.

San Martino (IGM sheet 122 Desenzano del Garda)

The Sardinian battlefield is nine kilometres south-east of Desenzano. It is accessible by bus and the A4 motorway, which passes just south of the railway line (PR2532), where Mollard rallied his battered division. A quiet minor road west of and parallel to the main Pozzolengo road leads up through vineyards past Monata Farm to Benedek's position on the high ground a kilometre to the south (PR2531). This features:

- Villa Contracania, the objective of seven separate attacks, and rebuilt after the battle. Stone plaques on the façade commemorate the villa's eventual capture, and surviving walls still show traces of the fighting.

- The 65m-high Torre Monumentale, on the site of the much-contested farm at Roccolo. This affords spectacular views of the battlefield. Frescoes within depict military scenes from the Risorgimento, including the assault on San Martino. Behind the tower a museum houses weapons, uniforms, and portraits. Both are open daily.

- The ossuary: previously a chapel of the Conti Tracagni, who owned Contracania, it houses the remains of several thousand men killed at San Martino.

- A minor road and path between points 101 and 110 follow the Austrian front line around the top of the hill.

Madonna della Scoperta is at the junction of IGM map sheets 122 and 143, the church itself appearing on the latter (PR2327). Fighting spread north-west onto sheet 122 square PR2129. The Piedmontese later advanced east along the Pozzolengo road to Bosco (PR2628). An *albergo* in the hamlet does an excellent lunch with local wine.

Milan and Brescia both have Musei del Risorgimento covering Italian unification from the 1790s to 1870, located at Via Borgonuovo and Brescia Castle respectively. Opening times of Italian museums vary, and it is wise to check in advance. The Milan museum's website is www.museidelcentro.ml.it.

FURTHER READING

Military accounts of the campaign in English are scarce. Absinthe Press of Minnesota USA and George Nafziger have both republished Colonel H. C. Wylly's *The Campaign of Magenta and Solferino* (London, 1907) in 1996 and 2008 respectively. Major Miller RA VC visited the battlefields, and wrote a *Study of the Italian Campaign in 1859* (Woolwich, 1860), recently reprinted by Ken Trotman. Miller's Royal United Service Institute lecture on the campaign appears in the *RUSI Journal* 1862 pp. 269–308. The most famous account is Henry Dunant's *A Memory of Solferino*, published by the International Committee of the Red Cross (Geneva, 1986).

A useful analysis in straightforward French is *Magenta et Solferino (1859) – Napoléon III et le rêve italien* (Economica, 1993) by Raymond Bourgerie.

Contemporary French language accounts include:
Baron de Bazancourt *La campagne d'Italie en 1859* (Paris, 1860) – written for
　　　　Napoleon III
F. Lecomte *Rélation historique et critique de la campagne d'Italie en 1859* (Paris,
　　　　1860) – by a Swiss army officer
L. Vandervelde *Précis de la Campagne d'Italie en 1859* (Paris, 1860) – by a Belgian
　　　　officer, including many official reports.

'A German View of the War' appeared in *United Service Magazine* (September–October 1859 pp. 27–41, and 207–17), while the *Edinburgh Review* (1859 pp. 454–94) contains an account by *The Times* correspondent at Austrian headquarters. His Allied counterpart's reports appear in *The War in Italy*, with Carlo Bossoli's coloured plates, (Day & Son, 1859). This recently reappeared in English and Italian as *La Guerra in Italia* (Point Couleur, 1996).

An invaluable modern work on the Austrian Army is M. Zannoni & M. Fiorentino *L'Esercito Austriaco nel 1859* (Editrice Militare Italiana: Milan, 1988). Simply written, it can be decoded with an Italian dictionary. The Societá Solferino é San Martino, who maintain the museums at those places, publish a beautifully illustrated *Guide to the Monuments of Solferino and San Martino*, which reproduces Sardinian official accounts and their order of battle.

For military railways, see E. Pratt *The Rise of Rail Power in War and Conquest* (London, 1915 & 1919), and Captain H. W. Tyler RE 'Railways Strategically Considered' (*RUSI Journal* 1864 pp. 321–43).

INDEX